Never the *Same* Again

Encouragement for new and not-so-new Christians

Shaw Clifton

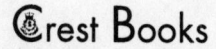

Crest Books

Salvation Army National Publications
615 Slaters Lane
Alexandria, VA 22313

© copyright 1997 The Salvation Army

All rights reserved. No part of this publication may be reproduced, stored in a retrieval system, or transmitted in any form or by any means—electronic, mechanical, photocopy, recording or any other—except for brief quotations in printed reviews, without the prior permission of the publisher.

Published by Crest Books
The Salvation Army National Publications
615 Slaters Lane
Alexandria, VA 22313

ISBN 0-9657601-0-3

Unless otherwise indicated, scripture taken from the HOLY BIBLE, NEW INTERNATIONAL VERSION. Copyright © 1973, 1978, 1984 International Bible Society. Used by permission of Zondervan Bible Publishers.

Unless otherwise indicated, all song quotations are taken from *The Song Book of The Salvation Army,* © 1987 The Salvation Army.

Printed in the United States of America.

I dedicate these chapters to Matt, Jenny and John.

Contents

Acknowledgements .... *vii*
Foreword .... *ix*
Introduction .... *xiii*

1. What Have I Done? 1
2. Can I Be Sure I'm Saved? 13
3. What Are the Ground Rules? 23
4. Can I Have A Role Model? 45
5. How Much Like Jesus Can I Be? 63
6. Will God Equip Me to Serve Him? 81
7. What Are the Gifts of the Spirit? 95
8. Will I Ever Be a Saint? 109
9. What About My Money? 125
10. Can I Witness? 141
11. What About My Job, My Studies? 153
12. Can I Really Rely on God? 165

Index *173*

Acknowledgements

Crest Books acknowledges the vision and insight of the USA Commissioners' Conference, and the contribution of the Eastern Territorial Literary Board, including territorial commander Commissioner Ronald G. Irwin and literary secretary Lt. Colonel William D. MacLean.

This is the initial offering of the Salvation Army National Book Plan. The plan's primary mission is to publish six books in a two-year period for distribution throughout the United States. The National Publications Department, under the leadership of Lt. Colonel Marlene Chase, working in conjunction with the author and book project manager Tim Clark, has made possible this landmark project that builds upon the Army's literary tradition.

Foreword
by General Paul A. Rader

With the publication of Lt. Colonel Shaw Clifton's helpful guide to the exciting walk of faith for born-again "becomers," the National Headquarters of The Salvation Army in the USA enters on a promising publishing venture. If the first offering is a foretaste of what is to come, Salvationists and friends of the Army can expect a soul-nourishing, "Body-building," down-to-earth diet of helpful materials to assist our spiritual growth. This useful clutch of chapters, so chock full of reliable guidance on the adventure of life in Christ, grew out of the author's informal chats with his own son. That lends Colonel Clifton's counsel a personal quality and practical value that makes it all the more relevant to those who can *Never* [be] *the Same Again,* because of their faith encounter with the Lord Jesus.

What the Bible means by "salvation" is not always readily grasped by those who have been immersed in a way of life so devoid of an awareness of God that one author calls theirs "a world without windows." God, for his part, wants to be understood. He wants his claim of love and offer of life to be perfectly clear. That is why the Eternal Word became a human person in Jesus and "moved into the neighborhood" (John 1:14, *The Message*), so that we could glimpse his glory and be gripped by the Truth. And it is why Shaw Clifton has provided for us this clear and helpful introduction to the way of salvation and the walk of faith.

Especially timely is his sound instruction on scriptural holiness. He explores what it means to enter into an experience of holiness that opens the door on the privilege and possibility of living a Christ-like life in a self-indulgent, soul-shrunken world oblivious to the grand reality of God's purpose and provision for the life beautiful. A life like Christ's.

It is a joy to commend this useful primer in Christian living, with the prayer that many will not only profit from it personally but will take the opportunity to share it with those whom they befriend and lead to faith in the Lord Jesus Christ.

International Headquarters
London
April 1997

Introduction

It is my prayerful hope that what is in these pages will help and encourage new Christians (and perhaps even some who may no longer be described as new) to become established in the faith.

The material is intended for readers of any age and, while written out of a Salvation Army background, of any denomination. Bible references are from the New International Version unless otherwise stated.

The choice of topics has been influenced strongly by questions put to me by my son, Matthew, in the course of long conversations during the last few years as he has come to the Lord. Then a student in London, he would meet me when work took me there. Many a meal in a Chinese restaurant became the setting for searching discussion, some of which is reflected here.

The manuscript was written in spare moments during a recent summer in England's famous Lake District, and at my sister's cottage in the English county of Somerset, a haven of quietness and peace.

Shaw Clifton
Boston, USA
Spring 1997

Chapter 1

A glance over your shoulder

What Have I Done?

Welcome!
Welcome! Nice to have you in the family—God's family, that is!

You've done a great thing. You have become a Christian, a follower of Jesus. Things will never be the same again.

Perhaps your journey into faith and to accepting Jesus as your own personal Savior has been a fairly long one. Perhaps you have had to overcome many obstacles or endure setbacks. Or maybe your stepping into faith has been just that—the making of what seemed simply a short step from unbelief to belief. Again, you may have come to Christ from having previously known very little about him, or you may have had a Christian family background. Anyway, you've done it!

Importantly, you've done it as your own choice, in your own right, as yourself. It is something no one else, not even Christian parents, could do for you. Yes, others could encourage you, pray for you or even plead with you. But only you could make that final choice to give yourself away to the love and lordship of Jesus. It is the best, the greatest thing anyone can do. And you've done it!

Goodbye Unbelief! Hello Faith!

Thank God that he has awakened in you a spark of faith. If you let him, he will fan it into a bright flame that will light up and warm your whole being and existence. You are going to meet people, however, who will simply not grasp what has happened to you. I hope you will never look down on them or despise them. That is unchristian. Love them for the sake of Christ and, if possible, befriend them.

Never forget that atheism (the belief that there is no God) and agnosticism (not knowing or not caring whether God exists) will always have their followers. Some will be uninterested in your own beliefs, but others will be aggressive and will actively try to pull you to pieces, seeking to demonstrate the foolishness (as they see it) of your faith in God.

I pray that you will be gentle and courteous at all times in your responses. Try to learn more and more about your faith and the teachings of Christianity. This book can help, as a start, in many ways. Read your Bible, develop your private prayer life and settle into a worshipping Christian community. Each of these things will help you to become strong and stable, given time. Later chapters have more to say about this.

You have taken a tremendous step forward in choosing Christ. His Holy Spirit is going to hold you day by day and will lead you gradually into more and more of the deep truths of the gospel (see John 16:13).

You are no longer in unbelief. You are a person of faith, even if for now you feel you're only a fledgling. You believe that God is real and that God is love (1 John 4:8, 16). God also is light (1 John 1:5) and he will enlighten you as you learn to be more and more open to him.

So, goodbye unbelief! Hello faith! Only fools say to themselves, "There is no God" (Psalm 14:1; 53:1). You are *not* a fool.

From "no people" to "God's people"

Why not look up right away what the Apostle Peter wrote? ("Apostle" means "one who is sent," i.e. sent by God.) Find 1 Peter 2:10. You can use the contents page at the front of your Bible for easy reference. Verse 10 states: "Once you were not a people, but now you are the people of God; once you did not receive mercy, but now you have received mercy." This applies to every Christian but is especially meaningful for a new Christian.

Peter knew that those receiving his letter were familiar with the history of the Israelite nation. In the Old Testament the Israelites are called to be God's chosen people. They adopted many customs and practices to symbolize this, but it was God's presence with them and among them that made them a distinct people. In Exodus 33:16 their great leader, Moses, speaks to God for all the people, saying that the divine presence "will distinguish me and your people from all the other people on the face of the earth." God had promised, "My Presence will go with you." Marvelous!

This same promise is for you. You are now one of God's people. In the New Testament book of Hebrews (chapters 7 and 8), written to the author's fellow Israelites, we meet the idea that God regards all who believe in Jesus as Savior as part of a new and sacredly binding relationship with God (a "covenant"). It is as though Christians are a new Israel, a new chosen people.

This thought brings encouragement. You are one of God's people, a distinctive people in his sight. Distinctive? Different? No doubt about it! You are saved, forgiven. You've seen yourself as a sinner needing forgiveness and have come humbly to Jesus to find it. Your seeking has been rewarded and your prayers answered. Old guilt has gone. You can, so to speak, look God in the eye and not flinch. You are now on speaking terms with him. You are at one with him. He has begun something in you which will grow and grow. You have committed your future to him in trust, and your eyes are on Jesus and heaven.

Never forget God's promise: "My Presence will go with you." You are distinct in his sight.

Coming home

This distinctiveness does *not* mean that God loves you more than he loves other people. He has no favorites. He loves indiscriminately. Because this is how God loves, he asks us to love both our friends *and* our enemies (see Matthew 5:44-48 and Romans 5:6-11). He loved you with an immeasurable love when you were unsaved and that is how he loves all unbelievers and unforgiven sinners still. Your coming into faith neither enlarges nor diminishes God's love for you. His love remains the same—unfathomable, freely given and endless. He loves us, sinner or saint. It is the sin he cannot tolerate.

Jesus teaches that God has an attitude of acceptance toward us. You have already sensed this for yourself. He is a waiting and welcoming Father. He longs for his erring creatures to come home. A famous hymn by Will Thompson shows Jesus in this light too:

Softly and tenderly Jesus is calling,
Calling for you and for me!
Patiently Jesus is waiting and watching,
Watching for you and for me!

Jesus drives home this truth in his story of the waiting father and the wasteful, foolish son. You can read it in Luke 15:11-32. The real hero of the story is not the runaway son, but his patient and loving father. When a wayward boy eventually staggered home, his Dad ran to meet and embrace him.

This lets us see how God feels about us. When you stepped out toward Jesus, your footsteps faltering, but the first real surge of saving faith driving you on, your heavenly Father saw you coming home. When you were still quite a long way off, he came to meet you, arms outstretched in welcome.

The story is told of a modern son who left home after a family argument. After a while he wrote home: "If you want me back, tie a handkerchief to the tree in the front yard and I'll see it from the train. Then I'll know either way." What a sight met his anxious, nervous gaze! Every handkerchief in the house decorated the tree! What a welcome home!

The flags of welcome are out in heaven for you. You have come home.

The cross of Jesus—surpassing your reason, but winning your heart

Now that you are a Christian, the cross of Jesus and all that happened at Calvary for you will never be far from your mind. The cross, you may find, will come to have an increasing fascination for you. Keep it *ever* in view.

For a moment, though, why not glance back over your shoulder and reflect on how you thought about Calvary and Jesus dying before you were saved? Maybe you gave it all very little attention. Or perhaps you experienced some curiosity, or a vague sense of interest and searching. It is even possible that you were quite well-informed about the New Testament narratives of our Lord's arrest, trial, suffering and execution. Nevertheless, none of what you knew touched upon your deeper emotions or spiritual faculties.

What a world of difference there is between head-knowledge and heart-knowledge. Even a grasp of the theological subtleties of the death of Jesus can leave a person quite unaffected personally, and far short of an inner spiritual commitment to Christ as Savior. How sad that this is so.

You, however, have begun in a clearly marked way to move from mere head-knowledge (interesting and useful in a way though this is) to a definite heart-knowledge of what happened on the cross.

Calvary cannot fully be explained by the historical facts alone. You know this now. You have begun to sense not just "what happened," but rather what "went on." By this I mean the deeper and underlying effects of what took place. You have seen in the events of Calvary something of profound and lasting significance for your own life.

Please do not be too frustrated if you find at first that you are a bit lost for words to express all of this. You are not the only one! Even experienced Christians struggle to express in limited human language the mysteries of the cross of Jesus. Keep reading your Bible and you will find there repeated and varied references to the cross and its significance.

It was George Carey, the present Archbishop of Canterbury, who wrote of the cross being like a matchless jewel. Turning it, you see one facet after another, each as beautiful as the last, but none adequate on its own to account for the total beauty of the stone.

So with the cross. No single explanation or theory can fully explain what went on. No particular theological insight can sum up all the depths of truth. You will hear from time to time various theories (known as atonement theories) about the ultimate meaning of the death of Jesus. Each can claim some New Testament support. Each is reflected in Christian songs and hymns. One theory regards the death of Jesus as a punishment suffered in our place, Jesus being our substitute. Another sees it as a ransom paid, another as a sacrifice to a righteous God. Some see it as the paying of an outstanding debt, and so on.

Do not get bogged down in all of this. Resist the fascination of the doctrinal conundrum for now and return to it later perhaps, if the desire to do so persists.

You could focus for the time being on simply thanking God for Calvary and for Jesus. Thank him that although these enormous events and their eternal significance surpass your reasoning powers, they have stirred and captured your heart.

It was General Albert Orsborn, a well-known Salvation Army leader, who wrote these verses about the cross of Jesus:

'Tis the end of my sin and the source of all grace;
'Tis the word of God's love to a prodigal race;
'Tis the greatest, the grandest gift God could impart,
Surpassing my reason but winning my heart.

O the charm of the Cross! How I love to be there!
With the love that shines from it, what love can compare?
The seal of my ransom in Calvary I see,
All my sin, O my Savior, laid upon thee!

It will help if you can spend some time finding statements in the Scriptures about the cross. For instance, Romans 5:8-9 speaks of the cross showing how much God *loves* us, and of our being *put right* with God by the death of Jesus. For Bible statements about the *healing* and the *forgiveness* that flow from the cross read Isaiah 53:5-10, Romans 3:25 and Ephesians 1:7. Also, try to locate Bible statements about the *victory* won by the cross. For example, Romans 6:10 refers to Christ's victory over sin. Colossians 2:14-15 paints a graphic picture of our Lord's victory over the forces of evil and

Hebrews 2:14 highlights his victory over death and the fear of death.

This last point is an interesting one. It has been suggested that the hallmark of a Christian is that he or she has no fear of death. This is worth thinking about. There may be some natural anxiety about the process of dying, but no fear of death itself. Certainly, I have met many Christians who knowingly faced death with complete calm, poise and assurance. My own mother was among them. When dying of cancer in 1984 she came across a verse of a Christian hymn that spoke of death. In the margin she wrote: "No fear at all."

May forgiveness, healing and victory be your experience too as you allow the Bible's words about the cross of Jesus to win your heart more and more. Where your heart goes, your reasoning powers will follow. It was the saintly Anselm of Canterbury (1033-1109) who said: "I believe, in order to understand" (*Credo ut intelligam*). It's a good way to go about things.

Born twice

Becoming a Christian, seeing how much we need forgiveness for our sins and finding this in Jesus and all he did at Calvary, is really a fairly straight forward thing. No one needs to be a genius in order to do it. Richard Jukes (1804-1867) wrote a much-used gospel song that put it like this:

The way to Heaven is straight and plain ...
Repent, believe, be born again ...

This last phrase, "born again," is often used in Christian circles. It comes from the words of Jesus recorded in

John 3. There we are allowed to eavesdrop on a night-time conversation between Jesus and a sophisticated Jewish religious scholar called Nicodemus. Jesus tells him that to see the Kingdom of God he needs to be "born again." Nicodemus is puzzled and asks how someone can re-enter his mother's womb and be born a second time! It is then that Jesus spells it out. This second birth is a spiritual birth, not a physical thing. The *Good News Bible* puts it like this: "A person is born physically of human parents, but he is born spiritually of the Spirit" (verse 6).

Receiving spiritual life in knowing Jesus as your Savior is as momentous an event as the day you were born into the world as a tiny baby. So someone who is saved as an adult, born again of the Holy Spirit at a mature age, is in fact at first just a baby in spiritual terms. It is pretty important to grasp this if you are a new Christian, so that you do not try to walk, so to speak, before you learn to crawl, or run before you can walk. Recognize your need to grow in your spiritual life and do not expect too much of yourself too soon. Later chapters come back to this.

You may hear references to "born again Christians" in the media or press. Sometimes non-Christians (and even some unwise Christians) use this expression to refer to Christians who take the Scriptures very seriously and who are regarded by some as narrow in their views. Just occasionally, the phrase is even used in an almost sneering way and as a put-down. If ever you hear this, remember that this is an abuse of a beautiful saying by Jesus. It is taking his words and debasing their meaning. In the true Biblical sense of the phrase, you cannot be a Christian at all unless you are "born again." To speak of "born again Christians" is therefore to use a tautology, like saying "wet water"!

If you are a Christian, you have been born again. If you have been born again, you are a Christian. It is as simple as that. Yet even in its simplicity we are dealing with a deep and lovely mystery. None of us can fully explain how spiritual birth occurs. It is all God's doing. Read Matthew 19:16-26. When the disciples of Jesus questioned him about being saved (verse 25), he looked them in the eye and replied: "With man this is impossible, but with God all things are possible" (verse 26).

He has made it possible for you! Just to realize this again is enough to make you want to fall to your knees and thank him over and over. As your heart fills up with gratitude and rejoicing, there is gladness in heaven too. Coming to Jesus is the best thing you have ever done.

You've made a start, a new beginning. What is next?

CHAPTER 2

Four helpful ideas from the Bible

Can I Be Sure I'm Saved?

Doubts are not unusual

Do not be too alarmed if you find yourself wondering if you are truly and properly saved. Many new Christians go through this phase not long after their first real rush of enthusiasm for Christ and the gospel.

Often this wondering is no more than the result of an intelligent and inquiring mind, coupled with a bit of self-doubt. What follows in this chapter can help to set your mind at rest. That, at least, is the aim.

Occasionally the Tempter bombards a new believer with such force that there is a real danger of doubts becoming a serious obstacle to progress. In this situation you need to be sure of two things: first, that you are clinging as closely as you can to Jesus—through much, and even desperate, prayer; and second, that you tell your mature Christian friends and leaders what is happening to you, so that they can help you through and surround you with the strength and protection of their own prayers. It would also be a good idea to use Ephesians 6:10-18 as a regular portion from God's word. It lists "the full armor of God so that you can take your stand against the devil's schemes" (verse 11).

Whether your doubts about the reality and validity of your conversion are mild and fleeting or strong and persistent, the Bible has things that can help bring you an inner rest about the issue. We turn to this now, and in a moment we will look more closely at four different ideas used in the New Testament. First though, a general comment about knowing for sure that we are saved.

Knowing for sure

If your conversion experience was an intense one over a short and measurable period of time, it is possible that it was accompanied by a fair degree of emotion. I know it was not entirely or exclusively an emotional thing. Your whole being was involved—mind, body, spirit, feelings, etc. Emotions may have played a part also if your journey into faith was longer and more gradual. The climax and clinching moment of your journey (if you like, the moment of arriving) may have touched deeply into the springs of your emotions.

This is as it should be. Very often the Lord reaches us and speaks by touching us in a way that stirs us to our foundations. How can such a thing not be emotional?

I wonder if you are finding now, as time passes, that the emotions involved in your conversion experience are wearing off. Be assured that this is normal. The Lord knows that we cannot live our lives on an unceasing emotional high. He wants you to rely less and less now upon your feelings. He still wants you to love and honor him above all else, but you can do this with a wholehearted love that does not require emotional intensity all the time.

Remember too that our emotions are not always reliable as a guide to truth, or even as a gauge to our spiritual health. So the question of being sure you are saved, of knowing beyond doubt, is not really a matter of how you feel at all. Your knowledge of what has happened to you is chiefly a matter of the spirit. I refer to that part of you which longs for God and can be satisfied only by God. Your spirit, in turn, can inform your mind that you are saved, and your mind, in its turn, can trigger feelings of gladness and thanksgiving for this fact.

What is most needful, then, for new Christians who begin to doubt their salvation, is reassurance that all is in fact well. Note now with the utmost care the next sentence. It is the Holy Spirit who brings this assurance to the spirit or heart of a Christian. The Bible makes this clear. In 1 John 4:13 you can read this truth: "We know that we live in him and he in us, because he has given us of his Spirit" (see also 1 John 3:24). Note and be helped also by verse 15: "If anyone acknowledges that Jesus is the Son of God, God lives in him and he in God." Say this aloud a few times and sense afresh how close the Lord is to you. He is closer than close, because he indwells you now.

Let's turn to four Bible ideas. These explain and illustrate further the work of the Holy Spirit in assuring us

that we are truly the Lord's:
1. Adoption
2. Sealing
3. Guarantee
4. First fruits

Adoption

Everyone can easily understand this. The very first sentence of this book welcomed you into God's family. John 1:12 states that all who receive Jesus and believe in him become God's children. This applies to you. You are God's child.

We see it again in Galatians 4:6 where Paul reassures the Christians in Galatia that they are genuinely the Lord's people and can know it by the Holy Spirit speaking clearly within them: "Because you are sons, God sent the Spirit of his Son into our hearts, the Spirit who calls out, 'Abba, Father.' So you are no longer a slave, but a son." Then follows a wonderful promise: "And since you are a son, God has made you also an heir" (verse 7). Memorize this verse, even both verses, and use them in prayer if doubts creep up to trouble you.

Other encouraging and reassuring words about your belonging to God's family as his child can be found in Romans 8:15 and Ephesians 1:5.

Many of these promises are expressed in terms of "sonship," giving perhaps a rather masculine feel to the theme. Do not be put off by this if you are female. It merely reflects the laws and customs of the times in which the New Testament was written, when the eldest son inherited from his father ahead of the other children. I like 2 Corinthians 6:18 which holds out the promise explicitly to sons and daughters of God alike: "I will be a Father to you, and you will be my sons and daughters, says the Lord Almighty."

So, whether you are a female or male child of God, be glad—be reassured.

Sealing

We move away from the symbol of family life now to enter the world of the law and legal procedures. While it is less common these days, there was a time when legal documents were authenticated by the seal of the person for whom the document was prepared. You held a candle to a stick of wax, letting the molten wax (usually red) drip onto the paper. Then a seal or signet ring would be impressed into the wax, leaving a clear image of initials or a coat of arms when the wax hardened. You may have heard the expression, "signed, sealed and delivered," meaning that something has been completed in all the required stages. The sealing procedure is that just described.

The New Testament speaks of the Holy Spirit being God's seal upon us, proving and validating that we belong to his Kingdom through his grace and favor, and our loving trust in Jesus as Savior.

This comes out clearly in Ephesians 1:13: "Having believed, you were marked in him with a seal, the promised Holy Spirit." The same thing is said in 2 Corinthians 1:21, 22: "He anointed us, set his seal of ownership on us."

So, be reassured. Be sure. Your faith in Jesus has

indeed opened the way for God, by his Holy Spirit, to mark you as his own possession. Be glad. Feel safe.

Guarantee

In addition to ideas from family life and the law, the New Testament borrows a concept from the world of business and trade. It is the idea of a guarantee. Don't think of this in the sense of a promise given by a store or manufacturer when you buy their product. Focus more on the idea of a down payment or a first installment, with full payment to follow.

We read in various Bible verses that God gives believers the Holy Spirit as a guarantee (or down payment) of much more to come. For instance, in Ephesians 1:14 (immediately after the "stamp of ownership" verse) where the Holy Spirit is spoken of as "a deposit guaranteeing our inheritance." The writer, Paul, is driving home his point by using a variety of illustrations. He knows that many of his readers in Ephesus will understand easily his parallel drawn from buying and selling. We can grasp it too.

The same comes through in 2 Corinthians 1:22. The Holy Spirit is God's guarantee in our hearts of all that he has in store for us. This is repeated in 2 Corinthians 5:5 where it is clear from the context (see verses 1-5) that what is come to us from God includes eternal life and heaven.

Once again then, let these promises from Scripture speak to you. Let them override whatever small doubts may linger on from time to time.

First fruits

The fourth image is drawn from farming and agriculture. Even if you have no more than an apple tree, you can get hold of this concept quickly. The first fruit to appear each season will tell you whether the rest of the crop will be good or bad. Romans 8:23 refers to the Holy Spirit as first fruits of a harvest. The Spirit is given to Christians as a sure sign of the good things that lie ahead of us if we walk the path chosen for us in Christ. Even Paul cannot find exact words for this. In verse 18 he settles for describing it as "the glory that will be revealed in us."

That is intended for you. The Holy Spirit is in you, indwelling you. Your body is his temple (1 Corinthians 6:19). Give thanks for this, and thank God too for the "glory" you have yet to see.

Constant reminders

How gracious God is to give you his Holy Spirit. How considerate too that he has prompted the Apostle Paul in his letters to use illustrations that pick up on the four most fundamental aspects of human society: kinship, law and order, trade and working the land. Everyone can readily relate to one or more of these pictures.

So it is that each basic facet of human life and society holds a reminder for you that you belong to God now that you are a Christian. Whenever you are among your own relatives, you can be reminded that you have been adopted into sonship or daughtership with God. Whenever you walk past a lawyer's office or see a legal document of any kind, it can remind you that you are sealed with God's stamp of authenticity and ownership. Each time you pay for something, remember that the Holy Spirit is your guarantee of much more yet to come from God. When you see a field of wheat or a tree heavy with fruit, call to mind the Bible's words about the Holy Spirit being the first fruits, a sign from God pointing to a great harvest of spiritual blessings up ahead.

Let's move on to think about a few absolutely basic things to help you get off to the best possible start.

Chapter 3

Four things you need to know

What Are the Ground Rules?

No new believer ever progressed to any great extent without paying attention to some basic rules. Years ago a young Christian minister called Timothy was reminded of this. More experienced in the faith than his young friend, the Apostle Paul wrote to him about a few basics of the Christian life. He likened it to running as a trained athlete in a race: "If anyone competes as an athlete, he does not receive the victor's crown unless he competes according to the rules" (2 Timothy 2:5).

The ground rules you need to understand from the start have to do with:
1. Getting to know the Bible
2. Learning to pray
3. Knowing where and how to worship
4. Beginning in practical Christian service

Exploring your Bible

God's chief way of teaching you and of communicating his will for you is through the Scriptures. A Christian who neglects the Scriptures will soon grow spiritually feeble. The Bible is God's instrument for speaking truth to you. At the same time, it is a sword in your own hand to use in battle when your soul is besieged by the forces of evil and the world (see Ephesians 6:17). So a failure to know the Scriptures will leave you floundering in two ways: it will seriously hamper you in hearing God speak and you will find yourself weaponless in the harsh arena of the everyday world.

It is essential therefore that you develop, from the start, a habit of opening your Bible daily and reading it.

Which version? Well, you have plenty to choose from! I recommend strongly a modern version to begin with. The *Good News Bible* (GNB) aims to use standard, everyday, natural English for maximum understanding of the text. It is sometimes referred to as *Today's English Version* (TEV). The *Contemporary English Version* (CEV), published by the American Bible Society, also aims for simplicity of language and style. The *New International Version* (NIV), used in this book, is also very widely used today. *The Living Bible* (LB) is a very free paraphrase of the original Old Testament Hebrew and New Testament Greek. It takes a few liberties with linguistic accuracy but also manages to convey the meaning quite graphically at times. That's true also of *The Message*, widely available in the USA and now gaining popularity in the United Kingdom. The *Revised Standard Version* (RSV) and the *New American Standard Bible* (NASB) are best for serious study since they remain closest in translation to the original languages, though the style is a little stiff at times. Finally, you should be aware of the *Authorized Version* (AV) or *King James Version* (KJV) produced in 1611 on the authority (hence its name) of King James I. The language is old fashioned, but exquisitely beautiful. Because it is so distinctive, it is often easy to memorize.

My best advice is that you use the NIV for now, looking perhaps occasionally at the KJV. Before making a final choice, do two things: check which version is used by the congregation at your place of worship and visit your nearest Christian bookstore to browse among their stock of Bibles. Ask for prices too!

Did you know that 90% of all households own a Bible? But only half of the people ever read it! Reasons given in one recent survey included: "lost the habit" (49%); "too busy" (35%); and "difficult to understand" (20%). Let none of these ever apply to you.

Your Bible is going to be your constant companion. Don't, for goodness sake, go around quoting it to everybody all the time. Instead, adopt a quietly diligent and humble attitude of wanting to read it, understand it and be fed spiritually by it. It is God's inspired and authoritative word to you. For this reason, carve out time on a regular basis to read it. Read it prayerfully, first asking God to speak to you as you read and to enlighten you by his Holy Spirit. Study it. Bring your intellect to bear upon it. Seek advice about useful yet straightforward study guides and commentaries.

Remember there is a difference between reading the

Scriptures for inspiration and studying them for information. Both approaches are valid, but know which you are engaged upon at any given time.

For inspiration in your early weeks and months as a Christian, read Mark's Gospel. It will give you a quick, vigorous overview of the main events in the life of Jesus. Then move on to the Gospel of John for a rather different account of his life and teaching. Revel in the words of Jesus as he declares who he is and why he has come from heaven. Then enjoy the three Epistles (letters) of John. They are quite short, but packed with spiritual food which a fairly new Christian can digest without too much difficulty. Next, get into the Acts of the Apostles. Follow the first Christians as they faced persecution, witnessed marvels by the Holy Spirit and boldly obeyed God's promptings to ensure the expansion of the Church. After that you should begin to explore the Old Testament. Genesis is an obvious starting point, and the Psalms will become, in time, a rich vein of blessing for you.

It cannot be stressed too much that sound and healthy spiritual progress is linked inseparably to feeding upon the written word of God. When Moses died and the Israelites needed another great leader to take his place, the Lord raised up Joshua. The Old Testament book of Joshua bristles with gripping narratives of the Israelites under his command. From the start, however, success was made conditional upon obedience to God's word and law, at that time confined to what we know now as the first five books of the Old Testament. It was to these that God referred when he spelled things out to

Joshua at the start of his leadership: "Do not let this Book of the Law depart from your mouth; meditate on it day and night, so that you may be careful to do everything written in it" (Joshua 1:8). Next God gave a promise: "Then you will be prosperous and successful."

It is possible to sense in these words from the Lord to Joshua something of a parallel for you as you set out on your Christian life. If you too learn to love and cherish God's word, if you honor him by being attentive to it regularly, and if you intelligently obey what he says to you as you read, then you will know spiritual progress and success.

A few years ago I heard an eminent senior officer of The Salvation Army speak about his love for the Scriptures. Commissioner Edward Read (now retired) told how, as a young man, he made a covenant between himself, his eyes and the Lord. He promised God he would read nothing upon rising each morning until he had first read the Scriptures. Think about that, and let it both challenge and inspire you.

Prayer—getting started

Two centuries ago James Montgomery, a Christian hymn-writer, penned these words:

> *Prayer is the Christian's vital breath,*
> *The Christian's native air*

He wanted to say how crucial he had found prayer to be to his spiritual existence. Prayer is exercise for the soul. It keeps you spiritually fit. Neglect it, and you grow flabby and listless.

In the same hymn we find this verse:

> *O thou by whom we come to God,*
> *The life, the truth, the way!*
> *The path of prayer thyself hast trod:*
> *Lord, teach us how to pray!*

Two reminders leap out at us here. First, Jesus was a man of prayer. If he needed spiritual exercise through praying, how much more do we! Second, all Christians need to ask the Lord to teach them how to pray. For a new Christian this is an essential request. You may make it many times. There is, in fact, no reason ever to stop asking God for this, no matter how long we have been saved. There is always more to learn.

The Bible says this in plain language: "We do not know what we ought to pray for" (Romans 8:26). So always stay humble about your prayer prowess. Never boast about any aspect of your spiritual life, but least of all about your abilities in the life of prayer. The Scriptures see a direct link between humility on the part of the one praying and the effectiveness of the prayer made: "If my people ... humble themselves, and pray and seek my face, and turn from their wicked ways, then I will hear from heaven, and will forgive their sin and heal their land" (2 Chronicles 7:14, RSV). The New Testament is just as clear: "Humble yourselves before the Lord, and he will lift you up" (James 4:10).

The wonderful thing to grasp from the outset is that every thought of prayer rising up in you is prompted by God. So there is nothing to be self-congratulatory about. God knows how we need help, and so "the Spirit helps us in our weakness ... the Spirit himself intercedes for us with groans that words cannot express" (Romans 8:26).

Whenever we pray sincerely, the Holy Spirit reads our hearts' desires and is our advocate, our spokesman in Heaven. So don't fret about being eloquent. The validity of a prayer does not depend on what is said, but on the faith and sincerity prompting it.

How often should you pray? "Pray continually" is the answer in 1 Thessalonians 5:17! Clearly this cannot mean being literally in a posture and attitude of conscious prayer forever! But it does mean there is never a time that is unsuited to praying. We can approach God at any hour, day or night. It also means that the whole tone of a Christian's life should be a prayerful one, the result of regular and intimate conversation with God.

You may hear some Christians who say the whole of life is a prayer and so they do not set aside planned time for deliberate and focused praying. This attitude is often a lame excuse for laziness in prayer. Do not copy it. Each day, make time for a conscious turning of your whole attention and being to God. Experiment at first to find the time of day that suits you best. Most believers use early morning or before going to bed. Many use both, and enjoy the benefits of this.

Where should you pray? In a place of quietness if at all possible. No TV or radio blaring! Try to be alone. If this is impractical at home, there may be a place out doors or even at work. Some people make a point of getting to work early in order to find quietness and privacy. If you are a parent of small children, you may experience real problems in finding either time or a quiet place, so ask other active Christians how they manage. Be inventive!

Keep your expectations of yourself low for now. There is much to learn and far to go. If you have an outgoing or extroverted personality, do not impose on yourself a strict regimen of an hour a day alone in silent meditation! This will take far too much out of you. You'll end up disappointed with yourself and discouraged. Do, of course, take some time to be alone with God, but also explore what openings may present themselves for praying in the company of a Christian friend, relative or colleague. A small prayer cell or group might also be a helpful setting. Be ready to experiment in order to discover what is best for you. You may also find it easier to say your prayers out loud, or to use devotional Christian music as you pray.

On the other hand, if you are a fairly self-contained or introverted person, praying aloud with others may be the last thing for you at this early stage. Avoid putting this sort of pressure on yourself. If you are content to spend substantial periods of time alone, then solitary prayer will come more naturally to you. The Lord knows we are all different and that we will respond in different ways. Be patient with yourself as you find out what suits you and your spiritual needs.

What should you include in your prayers? Well, remember that prayer is more than talking to God or formulating sentences either silently or aloud. Much of prayer can be silent waiting on God, listening for him to speak. He reaches us sometimes through a growing sense of conviction as we pray like this, or through a prayerful consideration of a passage or verse of Scripture. If, however, you address God in prayer using your own words, try to be reasonably ordered in the sequence of your thoughts. I list below some suggestions to guide you:

1. Speak words of *adoration* and try to *worship* God as you pray. Tell him you know and acknowledge who he is, your great and loving Creator, your heavenly Father.

2. Include words of *thanksgiving* for all his mercies to you. Most of all thank him for Jesus, your Savior, in whose name you are praying.

3. It is important to come before God without pretence, so be ready to *confess* with humility your wrong actions, words and thoughts. This will bring a sense of release.

4. Ask then for *forgiveness,* pausing to sense his touch on your soul, thanking him again for his patience and compassion toward you. Sense his healing power, his cleansing.

5. Now go on to make prayer requests. Offer *petitions* (requests) and *intercessions* (requests on behalf of others) for specific situations and for people you can bring to God by name. "The prayer of a righteous man is powerful and effective" (James 5:16).

6. Conclude by *offering yourself* again to him in the service of the gospel of Jesus. Tell him you want to be a useful, fruitful disciple. Ask him to guide your steps that day.

Should you use prayers written by other people? Yes, from time to time and as you come across prayers that strike a chord or raise an echo within you. There are some really good collections of prayers. Years ago my mother sent me a book of prayers by Professor William Barclay and wrote in it: "Sometimes you may be too tired to formulate your own prayers, so you can use these instead." I know now how wise she was in this.

Here is an example of a prayer I have used on countless occasions to start the day. It is by Charles Kingsley:

Stir us up to offer to you, O Lord,
our bodies, our souls, our spirits,
in all we love and all we learn, in all
we plan and all we do, to offer our
labors, our pleasures, our sorrows
to you; to work through them for your
Kingdom, to live as those who are not
their own, but bought with Your blood.
Amen.

Be confident that God hears your prayers. Remember what was said earlier about the Holy Spirit helping you to pray. Be on the lookout for positive results. You will notice, over time, that you are a stronger, healthier Christian if your prayer life is active and well-ordered. Also, you will long to see positive answers to your petitions whether for yourself or for others. Remember that, just like a loving human parent, your Father in heaven knows your needs. So, sometimes he answers with "Yes," sometimes with "No." "No" is an answer. There is no such thing as unanswered prayer. Again, God may answer with "Not yet." Be patiently persistent in prayer, never losing heart. Some have prayed for years and years before seeing a result. Finally, the answer might be "If ..." God may set a condition before he is ready to act. The condition may well have to do with your own closeness to him, or your own obedience to his will for your life.

Before examining briefly a third essential of the Christian life, let me say a word about the vast number of available books about prayer. Many are useful. Ask your Christian leaders for advice when choosing what to read. However, never make the mistake of thinking that reading about prayer is the same as praying. In the end, the only way to learn the art of prayer is to pray! Reading books on swimming may be okay, but you'll never swim until you jump into the water!

A place of worship

It is likely that you already have a link with a place of worship. If not, it is important that you become part of a Christian worshipping community. This gives you a setting for regularly worshipping God, hearing the Scriptures read and explained through the preaching, praying in the company of other believers and drawing strength through good fellowship. It also gives you a opportunity to make a contribution to the life of the church, the body of Christ on earth.

What sort of picture do you have of the Christian church? Try to see it as God sees it. I'm referring here not to any particular denomination, but to the body of all true believers in Jesus as their Savior, regardless of whether they are Baptists, Methodists, Salvationists,

Roman Catholics or other persuasions.

The Bible lets us catch some idea of how God thinks of the Church. Try reading 1 Peter 2, the whole chapter. Read it in a couple of different versions and look for the following pictures of the Church to emerge:

1. A crèche of infants (verse 2);

2. A temple of living stones (verse 5);

3. Priests at worship (verse 5);

4. A chosen race, a holy nation (verse 9);

5. Formerly no sort of people (once aliens and refugees), but now God's people (verse 10);

6. A fellowship of privileged sufferers (verses 19, 20);

7. A restored flock of lost sheep (verse 25).

The New Testament is filled with many different images of the Church, all true, and each one worth thinking about as you consider your own place and role in the church. As you decide which local place of worship to make your spiritual home, or reflect upon where you have already decided to belong, remember that God does not hold just one stereotyped notion of what his church on earth is. Here are some more Bible pictures of the church:

8. A community called out to be God's holy people (1 Corinthians 1:2);

9. A team of athletes (Hebrews 12:1, 2; 2 Timothy 2:5);

10. Citizens of heaven (Philippians 3:20);

11. A staff of faithful stewards (1 Corinthians 4:2);

12. A fellowship of babes in Christ (2 Corinthians 5:17);

13. An orchard growing spiritual fruit (Galatians 5:22);

14. A troop of Christ's soldiers (2 Timothy 2:3, 4)

It's a good idea to join the church through which you were led to Christ. If this is reasonably near to where you live, so much the better. Better still if you have already struck up a good rapport with the minister, pastor or officer in charge. It is not a good idea to postpone, month after month, the choice of where to worship God as a regular member of a congregation. Avoid drifting from church to church in aimless fashion. If you fall into this trap you will convey the impression that you are dodging the commitment involved in settling down as a responsibly-minded (though filled with joy!) new Christian. Whatever happens, do not get a reputation as a church hopper, someone who flits from church to church, sizing up the preacher and the preaching, and giving nothing back by way of commitment and practical service.

Think intelligently about why you are going to belong to your chosen place of worship. Be aware that the influences upon you may be those of family or of Christian friends. It could well be that the Lord will guide your choice through these very influences. Try, as time goes by, to reflect upon the things that have attracted you to your particular worship setting.

For instance, I am a Salvationist because of strong (and I believe God-directed) family influences, but also because I have decided for myself that I like the Army's simplicity and spontaneity in worship. I like too the combination of solemnity and quiet moments with happy, lively singing and music. I warm to the direct preaching and also the emphasis on evangelism. I confess I'm not naturally enthusiastic about wearing a uniform, but am glad to do so since it shows I am a Christian and it is my passport into the arena of ministry and witness God has chosen for me. Also, I highly value the Army's historical and prophetic witness to the accessibility and immediacy of grace without relying on external or sacramental rituals.

One very special reason why I am in the Army is because of the Mercy Seat, the focal place in Army corps halls where people can kneel in prayer, whether seeking Christ as Savior for the very first time, making some new or renewed commitment to God, or simply for quiet spiritual communion with the Lord from time to time. The Mercy Seat, being a meeting place between God and those who seek him, is the Army's heartbeat. (Read Exodus 25:10-22 for a description of the very first Mercy Seat, the "lid" or cover above the container for the stone tablets of the Ten Commandments. Note closely the promise in verse 22: "There ... I will meet with you.")

Once you are sure where you want to belong—and there are attractive things about each of the main Christian denominations—be diligent in your attendance. Just being present, especially on Sundays, is a tremendous encouragement to your leaders and other Christians. Excuses for not going will be easy to find. The Tempter knows them all! "Too much pressure on my time," "I must visit Auntie Millie," "I need a rest," "the services are boring" or "So-and-so has upset me!"

My great-uncle, Sam King, is now in Heaven. He used to attend The Salvation Army Sunday meetings in Goole, Yorkshire. When asked, on arriving home, if it had been a good meeting, Sam would reply: "Yes. It's always a good meeting, for there I meet with God."

Now Sam had learned a great thing. He'd learned to keep his spiritual eyes on Jesus, not so much on the leader or preacher, or on his fellow Salvationists. He knew why he was going to the meetings and when he got there he was able to exercise considerable skills as a worshipping member of a Christian congregation. This did not come overnight. It took time, experience and practice.

If you grasp at an early stage that just being in the congregation calls for certain skills, you will get more and more out of the services and meetings. Let me suggest a few skills that can, given time, make things much more meaningful for you:

1. Prepare your mind and soul for going into God's house by praying for the event you are about to attend.

2. When you enter the building and take your seat, silently lift up your heart to God to thank him that you are well enough to be there

(there are dozens too ill to attend but would love to do so). Thank him too for this place, his house, and for all your co-worshippers.

3. Consciously ask God to bless and help the leader and preacher, whose tasks are enormously difficult, though privileged and sacred.

4. Remain mentally alert throughout. Concentrate. Listen. Search for sources of surprise blessings in the words sung or spoken, also in the music.

5. Use your own Bible and follow whenever the Scriptures are read. Refer to it again as the sermon is preached.

6. Afterwards, think over what has happened. Try mentally to sum up in one sentence what God has said to you through the worship and praise. Tell him from your heart that you are truly grateful.

7. Resist strongly the temptation to pass negatively critical comments on the meeting or service, or any aspect of it. No meeting is perfect. No one pleases all the people all the time. Above all, never complain about the preacher or the message preached. God cannot bless you if your inner spirit is one of criticism or judgment. Remember that even the Apostle Paul was not particularly eloquent as a speaker (1 Corinthians 2:1-5), but God used him, contrary to merely human expectations. The day

might come when you stand before the congregation to speak. Then you will know how daunting it can be. Until then, your role is to pray the preacher through, respect what you hear, think it over intelligently as you listen, and try to be attentive. Your obvious attention will encourage and help your leaders. God will bless you for this; so will your leaders!

Make a point of getting on well with everyone in the congregation. Naturally, you will be drawn to your own age group, but be conscious of the need to have a word for everyone. Beware of being part of a clique. This can make for divisiveness which is contrary to God's will. First Corinthians 1:10-13 indicates this has been a problem in the church for centuries. Do not add to it.

Try not to judge your fellow Christians. As time goes by you will get to know many of them well. Some may share your outlook on life and even on matters of belief, but some may not. There is room for differences of emphases on non-essentials in church life. People are different, so make allowances. Be slow to judge others. Drink in the message of Jesus in the parable of the weeds (Matthew 13:24-30, 36-43) and realize that only God can judge the human heart with perfect justice. The Pharisees were quick to judge and Jesus did not like it (Matthew 9:9-12). Even the Twelve were prone to hasty, critical assessments (Luke 9:49-50; Matthew 15:23). So if they had to be wary, you and I must also be on our guard against this sin. It is important always to remember what you were before you were saved. That is the best safeguard against being a pious or self-righteous bore!

Some practical service for God

Everyone I have ever met who has just come into a new knowledge of the Lord has expressed an instinctive desire to do something for him. Nothing could be more natural. It is a loving and grateful response to the realization of all that Jesus has done for us at Calvary to save us from our sins.

I know a man who, on becoming a Christian, revelled in scrubbing the steps of the Salvation Army corps hall in Durham, England. I know another, in Newfoundland, Canada, who, when he could have been relaxing at summer camp, decided instead to clean out a grimy, old storeroom. He did it for Jesus.

Christians have before them a limitless range of practical things to do: sing in the choir, clean the church, arrange the flowers, sew, cut grass, do someone's shopping, write or mail letters for shut-ins, visit the sick, wash dishes, play in the band, gather or distribute hymnals, provide transportation on Sundays, bake cakes, keep in touch with missionaries, volunteer for nursery duty and a host of other opportunities.

The Lord, if you ask him, will open up an opportunity for you. Do not look for anything very public or high profile. That may, or may not, come later. If your service can be done so that few know of it, be glad. Never lose sight of the words of Jesus in Matthew 6:1-4. Why not look them up right away, before you read another sentence? There, you see—your heavenly Father sees what you do. That is enough.

Finding an outlet in this way is very Scriptural. I am thinking of what Paul wrote to the Christians in Rome about making their bodies available to God for practical and self-sacrificing service and about humbly fitting in (according to their gifts) with fellow Christians so that unity in the church would be enhanced. All this is in Romans 12:1-13. I like especially verse 11 (GNB): "Work hard and do not be lazy. Serve the Lord with a heart full of devotion."

Serve him also with an eye for detail. He is a God who notices details—details like you and me! Jesus missed nothing: crumbs (Matthew 14:20), hairs on our heads (Matthew 10:30), sparrows (Matthew 10: 29, 31). So if you are cleaning, do it thoroughly. If you are performing music, rehearse it meticulously. "Whoever can be trusted with very little can also be trusted with very much," said Jesus (Luke 16:10).

Should you ever grow weary in your service for the Lord or face discouragement, this prayer of Ignatius Loyola (1491-1556) may prove useful, especially the final two lines. Loyola was a military man before his conversion to Christ. He founded the Society of Jesus (Jesuits), and throughout his life was practical and down-to-earth.

Teach us, good Lord, to serve thee as thou deservest:
To give and not to count the cost;
To fight and not to heed the wounds;
To toil and not to seek for rest;
To labor and not to seek for any reward,
Save that of knowing that we do thy will.

We've considered four basic aspects of Christian life and service. Next on the agenda is the matter of role models. However, you will not go far wrong if you stick to the ground rules. What has been said here is only an outline, designed to help you make a start. If you get these things into place, "then you will be able to live as the Lord wants and will always do what pleases him," you "will produce all kinds of good deeds, and you will grow in your knowledge of God" (Colossians 1:10, GNB).

CHAPTER 4

Turn your eyes upon Jesus

Can I Have A Role Model?

Of course you can have a role model!
In fact, you can have several! Why not? We all have people who have inspired us. Some are figures from the past. Others are still alive, their example acting as encouragement. Some may be famous, some hardly known. What could be more natural, whether we think of our lives in general, or specifically of our Christian experience, than to have people to admire?

Now that you are saved, I recommend that you look afresh at those who draw your admiration. Now that you are a new creature in Christ your attitudes have changed. They will go on changing. Some characters who impressed you before may look pretty shallow now. You could begin by thinking of popular people in films, show business or the world of music. Some follow a lifestyle that is anything but Christian. Some worship money and possessions. Some have low sexual standards. Some abuse their bodies with drugs. Others drink to excess. Be realistic about these things and, as a result, be slow to give your admiration.

The same may apply to sports heroes. We marvel at their skills and prowess on the field or in the arena. But some of them stretch the rules to the point of cheating. Some indulge in violent outbursts. Others are foul-mouthed with their opponents, even with judges, referees and umpires.

Please understand what I'm saying here. I am most definitely not writing off the world of show business and entertainment, or of sport, as areas closed to Christians. I have my own likes and dislikes in these things—I still keep, and still enjoy, my old records from the swinging 60s! I have my favorite sports stars and the teams I support. Nonetheless, I have to be aware that even though I enjoy the music or, in sport, the competitive encounters, I need not be over-impressed by the lifestyles or role models offered by some of the individuals involved. Not if I am a new creature in Christ. Not, that is, if I've grasped what it means to see others and the world in general through Christian eyes.

That brings up another problem.

Current friends

You are likely to have several friends who are not Christians. What should you now do about that? Should you do anything at all? The answer is yes, you should. Just as I've suggested that you do an audit, as it were, of your worldly heroes, I recommend that you pause to think carefully and prayerfully about your friendships. This is a more serious matter than thinking about your heroes, for they are remote from you and are hardly likely to know if you show less enthusiasm for them.

When it comes to friends and social acquaintances, however, any change of attitude on your part will affect them directly. The first rule, then, is to remember that a Christian does not set out deliberately to hurt or upset anyone. All the same, something radical and life-changing has happened to you. You are no longer the person you were (2 Corinthians 5:17). Your whole outlook has altered (and will alter further still) and this is bound to have consequences. There may be people whose influence upon you has been bad and now you can see it. Do you want this to go on? Will you mix with them? Will you frequent the places they frequent?

Think about the people you regard as friends. You may want to distinguish here between real friends and mere acquaintances. Classifying people like this is, I know, a bit artificial, even a touch calculating. What you need to do, though, is to identify those relationships and social contacts which have been, and still could be, harmful to you. The Holy Spirit will give you insight about this if you calmly and sensibly place the matter before the Lord in prayer.

Here are some checklist questions to ask yourself:

1. Does this person share my faith?

2. Does this person feel comfortable with the fact that I am a Christian?

3. Does this person place obstacles in my spiritual path?

4. Does this person tempt me to do wrong?

5. Does this person draw me away from my place of worship and my service for Christ?

6. Does this person hold me back from some further commitment of my life and my talents to God?

If most of the answers come out on the wrong side, then clearly something needs to happen. A friendship that threatens to damage you spiritually cannot be allowed to continue as before. The important thing is knowing what to do about it. What do you say and how do you say it? Well, you may not have to say anything at all. There are ways of cooling things without being explicit or causing a confrontation. On the other hand, the Lord may lead you to speak quietly and gently with someone in order to explain exactly how you feel. This could lead to an upset or a misunderstanding, and you have to be ready for that. It's often a good idea to take more experienced advice first and there are Christian leaders who can give this. Do not act in haste; but do not dabble in dangerous liaisons either.

This whole matter brings up an age-old dilemma: how to sever an unhelpful friendship while at the same time leaving open a door of communication in case the other person becomes sensitive to your Christian influence. Again, prayer and advice will prove necessary. Sadly, there does come a point in many cases when the break must be made in order to protect yourself. Even after this, you may still be obliged to bump into your former companions: at school, work or in the neighborhood. The Holy Spirit will grant you both courage and wisdom in these circumstances. He will help you pray for them too. He may even, in time, revive the link and help you to lead a past friend to Christ. That is likely to be when you are stronger and more secure in your own faith.

An old gospel song by Richard Jukes puts the choice in stark and dramatic terms:
My old companions, fare you well,
I will not go with you to Hell,
I mean with Jesus Christ to dwell

A final word: if in doubt about the rightness of a relationship, pull out. Put your own spiritual well-being first. This is not selfishness, but spiritual self-preservation. Put another way, if you feel torn between a loyalty to old friends and a loyalty to Christ, remember who first loved you and gave himself for you. If the struggle seems impossible to resolve, look long and hard at 2 Corinthians 6:14-18 and the way may become clearer.

Heroes of the faith

A major source of inspiration for Christian living is found in the lives of great Christians through the centuries. Take time and energy to discover something of your spiritual forbears and your rightful heritage as a believer. You will be amply repaid for your efforts. There is literature galore, lots of it in fairly cheap paperback editions. If your explorations lead you occasionally to a more expensive volume, tell relatives and friends when it comes to birthdays and Christmas!

Here are a few "big names" to look out for. I'm putting them down in chronological sequence. This list mentions some people whose actions and writings have helped and motivated me. You will have your own heroes and heroines.

Anselm of Canterbury (1033-1109): He was an Italian Benedictine monk who eventually became Archbishop of Canterbury. I like his powerful mind. Most of all though, I like his willingness to trust God in faith when his human reason fell short. He was a man who yielded his intellect to God in all things. The result? God used him.

Francis of Assissi (1182-1226): Another Italian, famous for his simple lifestyle and his closeness to nature and the world of animals. He obeyed God's leadings, regardless of the cost. He was an all or nothing fellow. He said he was "married to Lady Poverty," the bride of Christ who had been a widow since Christ died. He loved his Lord so much that he spent endless hours in intense prayer. Few of us can emulate this and ought not even to try. Francis had a special gift from God in this regard. It is not for everyone, but his devotion can spur us on.

Martin Luther (1483-1546): One of my greatest heroes, Luther was the central figure of the Protestant Reformation in Europe in the early 16th century. A man of immense willpower and both physical and moral courage, he knew nothing of compromise when it came to matters of faith and the spiritual life. His vast output of literary works is still immeasurably influential upon millions today.

Teresa of Avila (1515-1582): A Spanish woman who battled in prayer for a close and mystical union with God. Her conversion sprang from the sight of a statue of Jesus after he had been whipped. This melted her heart. Many today still read her writings, even though they are highly individualistic (and not necessarily to be acted upon) with regard to the life of prayer. What I relate to best in her is her total capitulation to the suffering of Christ. It is a hard heart that can withstand the cross.

John Wesley (1703-1791): The leader of the Evangelical Revival in Britain in the mid-1700s. Raised in the Christian faith by his parents, he nevertheless came into a full experience of Christ for himself only as an adult and, moreover, 10 years after having been ordained. He was a powerful, articulate and enormously intelligent preacher. By journeying on horseback, he made the whole of England his parish. Often rejected by the so-called respectable churches, he rode on and preached on, even facing stonings, and was still preaching in the open-air when he was 87!

William Booth (1829-1912); *Catherine Booth* (1829-1890): They became the founders of The Salvation Army, coming from strong Methodist (Wesleyan) roots. Both had strong wills and personalities. Both were notable preachers. Like other great Christian pioneers, they obeyed God implicitly, regardless of cost. They broke new ground in actively promoting the ministry of women, a full century before it became a fashionable issue for debate in the churches. They were also ahead of their time in perceiving the dangers to life of tobacco and alcohol. Before the Booths, evangelicalism did not know how to combine spontaneously soul-winning and social work (social action, too) on a large scale.

Carvosso Gauntlett (1892-1951): An officer of The Salvation Army and the Army's foremost pacifist. He was the Army's Editor-in-Chief throughout World War II (1939-1945) and then led the Army in Germany once peace was restored. A man of enormous moral courage. Most Salvationists are not pacifists, but Gauntlett was not deterred by this.

Albert Schweitzer (1875-1965): One of the most famous Christians of the 20th century, he was also one of Europe's greatest intellectuals, holding doctorate degrees in music, theology and medicine. He founded the famous hospital at Lambarene in the Congo, and spent most of his adult years there serving the local population and their health needs.

Martin Luther King, Jr. (1929-1968): A Christian pastor and social activist in the USA who led

American blacks in a non-violent, nationwide campaign for civil rights. A passionate and noble-minded preacher, he was shot dead by opponents in Memphis. His inspiring influence lives on. He knew how to apply his beliefs to the social problems of his country and culture, all too rare a gift.

Just like the never-ending debate about, say, the best football players or the all-time greats of baseball, so there will never be agreement about our greatest Christian heroes and heroines from history. That is part of the glory of the Church through the ages. God can use these saints from both the distant and recent past to show us the heights of spiritual achievement and devotion which are open to mortals like you and me. Just remember, though, great as they were, they cannot replace Jesus in our lives. They may be fine examples to look up to, but they cannot save us from our sins. Only Jesus can do that. Let's keep this very much in mind as we look next at a few Biblical role models, for here again, even though we are considering mighty warriors for God recorded in Scripture, none of them can match Jesus. After all, they're dead! Yet Jesus lives!

Biblical role models

The Scriptures abound with details of men and women whose courage and daring for God quicken our pulses as we absorb the Biblical narratives. There is little need for me to say much here about them, for you can explore the Bible's accounts for yourself. Make sure you do. Do not settle only for second-hand versions in books *about* the Bible. Go also to the primary source for your information and inspiration. Read the Bible itself (see chapter 3).

Do not neglect the Old Testament. As you follow the ups and downs of Moses (God's great servant and leader), or of David (God's great shepherd and king), or of Isaiah (God's great statesman and prophet), you can develop a love for this part of God's word. Too often we forget to turn to its pages to listen for God's voice. Focusing almost exclusively on the New Testament will deprive you of much. Read up on Joshua, for example, God's great soldier and tactician. Note the closeness of his relationship to God and the detail recorded in Joshua 1:1-9 which contains God's timeless promise: "I will be with you; I will never leave you nor forsake you" (verse 5).

As you grow more fully acquainted with these figures from Israel's history, it will strike you just how very human, and in some respects how very ordinary, they were. Each had weaknesses and needs. Yet God could, and did, use them. This encourages us, for we are vulnerable and fallible too.

Job is another example. He was faithful to God, even in deep and extreme suffering, but eventually gave in to despair and tried to call God to account. In the end, though, he got back on track, having come to understand anew his place in the overall scheme of the universe.

You will notice the same combination of human frailty and notable courage in Elijah (see 1 Kings 18-19). He was capable of breathtaking feats for God, facing the risk of public ridicule and even death at the hands of the notorious Queen Jezebel. At the same time he knew exhaustion of both body and spirit, and was capable of deep pessimism. Still, God used him. Again, we can take heart from this.

There are amazing women, too, in the Old Testament who draw our admiration. The book of Ruth comes at once to mind. Notice her intense loyalty to her mother-in-law and her sense of family obligation. Esther is another. She is one of the heroines of the Jewish people, risking her life to rescue her fellow-Israelites from the destruction planned for them by Haman, a royal favorite.

Many of the New Testament personalities are just as intriguing. The four Gospels offer glimpses into the personalities of the twelve disciples. You must not expect to find 12 perfect people. Some were ambitious or lacking in faith, and all of them were slow to understand the mission of Jesus even though he taught them himself. You and I are therefore in good company!

Roam beyond the Gospels into the Acts of the Apostles. Here are accounts of the main events in the lives of the earliest Christians who responded to the promptings of the Holy Spirit to take the good news of Jesus far beyond the land of our Lord's birth. Notice Peter, who took charge of things at first (Acts 1:12-26). This is the same Peter who had earlier denied being linked with Jesus at all (Matthew 26:69) and yet was destined by God to be the "rock foundation" of the Church (Matthew 16:18). Think about this and realize sensibly that today's religious leaders are also flesh and blood. Their struggles and temptations are as real as yours. That is why they need your prayers and encouragement.

Peter's history shows too that even when we have let our Lord down pretty badly he can use us again if we are truly sorry—sorry enough to admit it and come humbly seeking forgiveness. John Gowans, who has written many songs used in Salvation Army circles, wrote these lines with Peter in mind:

Knowing my failings, knowing my fears,
Seeing my sorrow, drying my tears,
Jesus recall me, me re-ordain;
You know I love you, use me again.

I have no secrets unknown to you,
No special graces, talents are few;
Yet your intention I would fulfil;
You know I love you, ask what you will.

Words like these can be used in our own prayers when occasion demands.

Of all the early Christians, the example of Stephen impresses me most. You can read about him in Acts 6-7. He was handpicked for practical work in the Christian community. He was "full of faith" (Acts 6:5), "full of God's grace and power" (verse 8), "full of wisdom" (verses 3, 10), in short, "full of the Holy Spirit" (verses 3, 5). He was also articulate for God. Read his speech in Acts 7, delivered in front of powerful and intimidating people. His words were Spirit-inspired. "But the Spirit gave Stephen such wisdom that when he spoke, they could not refute him" (Acts 6:10 GNB). He addressed them courteously as "brothers and fathers" (Acts 7:2), but he spared them nothing as he reminded them of their spiritual history and their disobedience to God. From verse

51 on he demands a response and applies his message to his present hearers in the most direct and challenging way. Read his words aloud for yourself and hear them ring with disturbing conviction. They could not tolerate Stephen's accusation that they had murdered God's "Righteous One," Jesus (Acts 7:52), so they stoned him. Even as he died, he emulated his Lord in his words (verse 60). Full of faith, power and wisdom. Full of forgiveness too.

Stephen, the first Christian martyr, is one of the most worthy of New Testament role models. Notice who was present at his execution, holding the overcoats of those who were stoning Stephen. It was a young man named Saul (Acts 7:58; 8:3), later to become the great Christian teacher and apostle (or "sent one"). When Saul was converted (see Acts 9:1-9) he changed his name to Paul (Acts 13:9), symbolizing his changed life and beliefs. No silent or secret following for him.

I hope I have said enough to whet your appetite for finding out more about the role models offered to you in the women and men of faith found in the Scriptures. Take comfort from their imperfections; find inspiration in what they accomplished for God when at their best.

After all is said and done, however, there is only one role model who has the right to expect our best and undivided attention, and that is Jesus.

Your ultimate role model

Jesus is unique. There has never been, there is not, and there never will be another like him. When we think of the giants of history such as Alexander the

Great, Napoleon, Winston Churchill, or of the great intellects of our race like Confucius, Einstein or Shakespeare we find instinctively that we cannot place Jesus in lists like these. One Christian writer, Carnegie Simpson, puts it this way: "Jesus is not one of the group of the world's great ... Jesus is apart. He is not Jesus the Great; he is Jesus the Only. He is simply Jesus. Nothing could add to that." The well-known English poet, Charles Lamb, makes the same point, but more graphically: "If Shakespeare were to come into this room we would all rise up to meet him, but if that Person (Jesus) were to come into it, we would all fall down and try to kiss the hem of his garment."

The Scriptures bear this out. "Salvation is found in no one else, for there is no other name under heaven given to men by which we must be saved" (Acts 4:12). "God placed all things under his feet and appointed him to be head over everything for the church, which is his body, the fullness of him who fills everything in every way" (Ephesians 1:22, 23). This statement about the uniqueness of Jesus is beautifully retranslated by J. B. Phillips: "God has placed everything under the power of Christ and has set him up as head of everything ... He is the one who fills the whole wide universe."

How on earth, you ask, can someone who is unique become a role model? Surely, by definition, we simply cannot be like him!

How right you are. You will never be like him, not in the sense that you can try to copy other role models. But Jesus can do what no other role model can do for you. *He gives himself to you.* That is how you become like him. His Spirit lives within you. Any hint in a believer of Christlikeness, any small indication of goodness or purity, is not the result of the believer's effort to copy, but the outcome of the believer's willingness to receive from Jesus something of himself. The only limit on this is your capacity to receive him. Pray, therefore, for more and more capacity to receive him.

Here is my prayer for you, the reader, as you begin to realize how beautiful in character you can become at the hands of Christ. It is a prayer the Apostle Paul prayed for the Christians who lived in Ephesus (see Ephesians 3:16-19, GNB):

> *I ask God from the wealth of his glory to give you power through his Spirit to be strong in your inner selves, and I pray that Christ will make his home in your hearts through faith. I pray that you may have your roots and foundations in love, so that you, together with all God's people, may have the power to understand how broad and long, how high and deep, is Christ's love. Yes, may you come to know his love—although it can never be fully known—and so be completely filled with the very nature of God.*

Notice that these words from the Bible envisage the actual possibility of being completely filled with the very nature of God! This takes us to the heart of what it is to be Christlike, to be a mature yet still growing Christian.

This lovely process that happens to a believer is referred to also by Paul in 2 Corinthians 3:18 (GNB) in equally startling terms: "All of us, then, reflect the glory of the Lord ... and that same glory, coming from the Lord, who is the Spirit, transforms us into his likeness in an ever greater degree of glory." At first your capacity to receive him in this way is fairly limited but there is nothing to prevent it from increasing rapidly. Make this your prayer. Remember also that the more time you spend quietly with him, the more you will grow like him. You will find yourself seeing the world and other people more and more through his eyes. Your thoughts will be more and more his thoughts (see Philippians 2:5-11).

> *Turn your eyes upon Jesus,*
> *Look full in his wonderful face,*
> *And the things of earth will grow strangely dim*
> *In the light of his glory and grace.*
> —Helen H. Lemmel

His glory and grace can and will be evident in your life. His Spirit is alive and at work in you already. With humility and honesty on your part about your need, let him do his work. Let him cultivate in your personality those life-enhancing fruits which are called the "fruit of the Spirit." They are listed for us by Paul in Galatians 5:22 and are worth memorizing:

1. Love
2. Joy
3. Peace
4. Patience
5. Kindness
6. Goodness
7. Faithfulness
8. Gentleness/Meekness
9. Self-control

The whole of chapter five is devoted to looking briefly at each of these. Taken together, they are a portrait of the character of Jesus. Hence their central significance to you or to me as we pray for more and more of his likeness and his life within us. If you want these things, (and how can any Christian not want them?) remain open and teachable, for the Lord "will beautify the meek" (Psalm 149:4, KJV).

CHAPTER 5

Nine ways to be like Jesus

How Much Like Jesus Can I Be?

The Holy Spirit—your courteous, gentle helper

To understand more fully what the Holy Spirit does in the life of a Christian, and before we look in more detail at each of the fruits of the Spirit, it will help to say some general things.

For instance, who is the Holy Spirit? Think of him as the Spirit of Jesus, alive in every true believer. The Bible uses various names (see Romans 8:9-11) such as "God's Spirit," "Spirit of Christ" or simply "the Spirit" to mean one and the same—the Holy Spirit. Christian teaching about God includes the doctrine of the trinity, that God is three-in-one: Father, Son and Holy Spirit. The Holy Spirit is therefore not an "it" or a "thing." He is personal, just like our heavenly Father, or like Jesus, and so we speak about him as we would about any living person.

Why is the Holy Spirit described as courteous and gentle? This is something the New Testament shows with special clarity. If you had lived in Old Testament times, you would have thought of God's Spirit as rather impersonal, pretty awesome and even a bit frightening. Gideon (Judges 6:34, GNB) was a fairly ordinary guy until the "spirit of the Lord took control" of him. The original Hebrew in this phrase conveys the idea of the spirit of God "leaping upon" Gideon! The same comes across in Judges 14:6 where suddenly the Lord "came upon him in power" making Samson strong so that he began to do extraordinary things. The Spirit of God also "came upon" (literally: "leaped upon") David when he was anointed by Samuel as king (1 Samuel 16:13). Elijah (see 1 Kings 18:12, 46) gets propelled around from place to place when the power (spirit) of the Lord came upon him! In the light of New Testament insights this strikes us now as strange.

Above all else, the Holy Spirit's task is to focus attention on Jesus (John 14:26; 15:26; 16:12-14). John the Baptist did this (John 3:30) because he was "filled with the Holy Spirit" (Luke 1:15). When Jesus was baptized in the River Jordan the Holy Spirit was described as coming upon him "like a dove" (Mark 1:10). Doves are the gentlest of creatures. They symbolize peace and tranquility. The Holy Spirit acts in this way. There is nothing to fear. He is like Christ, whose feet were nailed down and broken for us. Feet such as these do not kick us into submission. He is not a bullying spirit. His method is love.

Mentioning love brings us back to "the fruit of the Spirit." This phrase from Galatians 5:22 (see various translations) can be used with the word "fruit" or "fruits." In English, "fruit" can be either singular or plural. The original Greek of the New Testament can be translated either way without damaging the meaning of the verse. There is no special doctrinal significance in saying either "fruit" or "fruits." Notice that the Good News Bible avoids all this by saying simply: "the Spirit produces ..."

Let us consider each of the fruits in turn. Each is a way of being like Jesus. None is an optional extra. Every Christian should have all of the fruits in their life, to one extent or another. The more mature a Christian is, the more evident these things will be. Try not to think of a bowl of fully-ripe fruit, juicy and polished, begging to be picked up and eaten at the whim of the chooser. Think rather, when you ponder the fruit of the Spirit, of a small bud or tentative blossom that will slowly but steadily grow and grow into the fullness and maturity of the finished product.

Love

Being loving comes first in the list in Galatians 5:22. This is not an accident. Love is the starting point from which all the other fruits grow. Take away love and all the fruits are strangled at birth. This love is not the sexual or romantic love felt between a man and a woman, or even the love which is shared in a family. It is the kind of love God has for you and me. The Bible has a distinctive Greek word for it—*agape* (pronounced: ag-a-pay). This is used every time the New Testament speaks of God's love for us. So it is a supernatural love which the

Holy Spirit places within us. It goes on loving even if it is not returned, like God's love went on and on, even in the face of the rejection and crucifixion of Jesus.

The centrality of *agape* love in a Christian's life is spelled out for us in Colossians 3:12-14 where Paul speaks of compassion, kindness, humility, gentleness, and patience, but goes on to single out love: "And over all these put on love *(agape), which binds them all together in perfect unity.*" This is why the great preacher, Dr. W. E. Sangster, wrote that "love is all the fruit in one." Pray then that the Holy Spirit will make you more loving: toward God, toward your fellow Christians and toward persons as yet unsaved. The practical consequences of this? No storing up grudges, no refusing to forgive, no moodiness, more acceptance of people as they are and a greater readiness to see what someone could become in Christ. How are you doing so far?

Joy

The New Testament is a book of joy. The verb, "to rejoice," and the noun, "joy," taken together crop up no less than 132 times! This joy is not some surface or temporary brightness of mood. Neither is it a general light-heartedness, or even a sense of optimism. Instead it is a deep-seated, inner state of ongoing spiritual gladness, the seed of which is implanted in us by the Holy Spirit when we are saved.

Paul knows that such joy is a special mark of being a Christian, the hallmark of any person who is, like you, in union with the Lord. Try searching out the 15 references to "joy" or "rejoice" in the letter to the Philippians, and sense the extent to which the whole document is an epistle pulsating with joy! Two of the four Gospels begin and end with joy (see Matthew 2:10; 28:8 and Luke 2:10; 24:52) as if to signal that the joy we know as Christians is inextricably bound up with the coming of Jesus and with his life, death and resurrection.

You know for yourself the joy, the deep gladness of heart and soul, that floods over a person when they receive Christ as Savior. The same joy is recorded in the New Testament when Zachaeus welcomes the Lord (Luke 19:6); it is there again when Philip's preaching is well-received in Samaria (Acts 8:8); and Paul is pleased to remind the believers in Thessalonica that when they first believed they "welcomed the message with the joy given by the Holy Spirit" (1 Thessalonians 1:6). I hope and pray that you also will know before too long the joy to be had in sharing the gospel news with others. The disciples of Jesus discovered it (Luke 10:17), and Paul actually calls those saved through his ministry "my joy and crown" (Philippians 4:1, KJV).

One final point. Because the joy which is planted and nurtured in you by the Holy Spirit is a supernatural thing, no human being can rob you of it (see the words of Jesus in John 16:22). Your joy, therefore, can survive disappointments and frustrations, even circumstances of suffering or persecution, as did the joy of the Christians in Antioch despite efforts to suppress the gospel (Acts 13:52). Notice, above all, the example of your ultimate role model. The writer to the Hebrews (12:2) speaks, in the same breath, of Jesus enduring the cross and of the joy that he knew in doing so.

Pray for a capacity to know an even deeper joy as you grow in the Lord. Be encouraged that Jesus prayed for *his* joy to fill those who believe in him (John 17:13). Let me add my prayer, using Paul's words in Philippians 4:4 (GNB): "May you always be joyful in your union with the Lord. I say again: rejoice!"

Peace

There is not a book in the entire New Testament that does not make reference to peace. Too often we think of peace in a shallow way, imagining it to be merely the absence or cessation of strife. When a war ends, the newspapers will print headlines about peace breaking out! The same when a trade union strike is over! Peace in this sense may mean no more than an uneasy truce or a stalemate, a stand off. This is not what the New Testament means by peace. When Jesus, about to face death, told his disciples: "Peace I leave with you; my peace I give you" (John 14:27), was he making them a passive bequest of simply no conflict, no strife? Was he handing on an uneasy spiritual truce? Nothing of the kind! He was granting to them a gift so infinitely precious that no one else in all creation could give it. It is offered now to you as a fruit of the Holy Spirit. It is the priceless experience of being in a right relationship with God, with yourself, and hence with others. It is a very positive thing. It is harmony. It is God striking the right chords within you so that you feel at ease with yourself—not complacent; just content to be you and glad to be a steadily growing follower of the Lord. Only a person thus at ease can be relaxed and in harmony with others. The Hebrew greeting, *"shalom,"* comes close to this idea, wishing another the experience of a life in harmony.

"Peace" is also a Christian greeting. It is Christ's resurrection greeting (John 20:21). It is in fact a common New Testament greeting. Check this in the opening verses of, for example, Romans and Galatians. Notice where the peace comes from: "from God our Father and from the Lord Jesus Christ." For you it is mediated from the same divine sources through the gentle, courteous ministrations of the Holy Spirit. In practical terms, you should now be easier to live with than before!

You cannot win peace by struggling for it or grasping after it. As with all the fruits of the Spirit, it is given, not seized. It is received, not achieved. Like joy, it can exist and continue in the believer despite trouble. Try to learn something about Dietrich Bonhoeffer, a notable German Christian who opposed Hitler. Read of his execution by hanging in 1945 in the prison at Flossenberg, but note carefully the testimonies of those who shared his final moments. They witness to his calm, tranquil spirit. He sought to comfort them in their distress at losing him. Now, who does *that* remind you of?

Yes, of Christ. Christ is our peace (Ephesians 2:14). Like the bumper sticker says, "No Christ, no peace. Know Christ, know peace." So as you pray to know more of Christ and of his indwelling, your knowledge and experience of his peace will deepen. Time and again you may feel that something or someone threatens your inner peace. That is when you must speak the name of Jesus in prayer, turning consciously and instinctively (the two are not mutually exclusive) to him for safety and a restored, renewed sense of peace.

Horatio Gates Spafford is not a name I would like to have, but heaven knows I long to possess completely the wonderful experience of God's peace he points to in his much-loved hymn:

When peace like a river attendeth my way,
When sorrows like sea-billows roll,
Whatever my lot, thou hast taught me to know
It is well, it is well with my soul.

Though Satan should buffet, though trials should come,
Let this blest assurance control,
That Christ hath regarded my helpless estate,
And hath shed his own blood for my soul.

For me be it Christ, be it Christ hence to live;
If Jordan above me shall roll,
No pang shall be mine, for in death as in life,
Thou wilt whisper thy Peace to my soul.

Patience

Being patient is probably one of the most elusive of the fruits of the Spirit. Some people are patient by nature. Here, however, the Bible is referring to God, through the Holy Spirit, placing within the believer something of his own divine longsuffering and forbearance. Martin Luther (see chapter 4) was anything but a naturally patient man. He knew full well the contrast between his personality and the longsuffering personality of God when he wrote: "If the world had treated me like it treated God, I would long ago have kicked the wretched thing to pieces!"

Quite so! God is not like us! Putting this in day-to-day practical terms, the fruit of divine patience in you, perhaps only a tiny glimmer at first, will curtail your short-temperedness. It will, through God's grace, keep you steady under provocation. The patient Christian is one who holds back from exasperation or retaliation (see Christ's example referred to in 1 Peter 2:23) whereas before he would not. God has been like this with you in waiting patiently to win you to himself. Paul, in Romans 2:4, writes of God's "kindness, tolerance and patience" in leading us to repent. This aspect of God's character is vividly brought out by Jesus in his story of the lost and wayward son in Luke 15:11-32. The real hero of the story is the father, who represents God. He waited patiently for his foolish son to come home (the son represents you and me) and welcomed him lovingly when the time came. It is very apt, therefore, that the famous German theologian, Helmut Thielicke, should call this story "The Parable of the Waiting Father."

To see this divine fruit of patience growing in the personality of a naturally impatient person is a remarkable thing. It is a sure indication that the Holy Spirit is at work in that person. So pray (patiently!) for more of this fruit from God. Then you will be "completely humble and gentle," you will be "bearing with one another in love" (Ephesians 4:1, 2). Notice here the link with love. Again, love is the ground of all the fruit of the Spirit, for "love is patient" (1 Corinthians 13:4).

Kindness

Not only is love patient, love is also kind according to 1 Corinthians 13:4. Dr. Sangster saw kindness as "love in its smaller manifestations." Being kind, at the insistance of the Holy Spirit, is therefore not about indulging others or pandering to their wants and wishes. It is rather to discern their needs and to respond in a way best suited to their long-term betterment.

Paul, in Ephesians 4:32, sees a close connection between kindness and being "compassionate," that is, sensitive to the needs of others, and even to their weaknesses so that kindness will flow over into forgiveness if necessary.

It is worth looking at the broader context of Ephesians 4:32 because it paints a picture of the Christian life, showing what must go out and what should come in when we follow Jesus. The following 13 things have to go:

- worthless, futile thoughts (v. 17)
- stubbornness, or hardness of heart (v. 18)
- vice and all sorts of indecent things (v. 19)
- the old self (v. 22)
- deceitful desires (v. 22)
- telling lies (v. 25)
- anger that leads into sin (v. 26)
- giving the Devil a foothold (v. 27)
- theft (v. 28)
- harmful, unwholesome words (v. 29)
- offending the Holy Spirit (v. 30)
- bitterness, rage, anger (v. 31)
- insults and hateful feelings [malice] (v. 31)

Which of us could manage such a cleansing for ourselves? A spring cleaning like this is a task for the Holy Spirit, who alone can then add to our lives the following adornments:
- the life that God gives (v. 18)
- the truth that is in Jesus (v. 21)
- a new mind (v. 23)
- the new self (v. 24)
- God's likeness (v. 24)
- the true life that is holy and righteous (v. 24)
- telling the truth (v. 25)
- working for an honest living (v. 28)
- helping the poor and needy (v. 28)
- helpful and encouraging words (v. 29)
- kindness, tender-heartedness and compassion (v. 32)
- forgiveness (v. 32)

Notice how this list starts with the life God gives and the truth that is in Jesus and gradually moves on into specific actions and attitudes. Right belief leads to right living.

Goodness

Sometimes we meet a person who is filled with goodness. Catherine Baird was a Salvation Army writer and poet. We were her neighbors and got to know her well. She would never in a million years have claimed to be good. But she was! There was something that was godly about her, but it came across in anything but a pious way. She was thoroughly realistic about people and their foibles, yet seemed able to love and accept all types. Everyone felt accepted, even esteemed, by her.

This made you want to be a better person and that is precisely the effect Jesus had on people. So Christ's Spirit was in Catherine Baird, making her good and godly. She was given also to acts of personal kindness. I think of this when I read the definition of goodness by a former Salvation Army world leader, Frederick Coutts, who said goodness is "love with its sleeves rolled up."

Catherine Baird also laughed a lot. Her eyes laughed, sometimes knowingly, even mischievously, but somehow you knew that from deep within there came welling up a joy and goodness that was of God.

I've offered this brief pen-portrait of a Christian lady because goodness is easier to describe than to define. We know it when we meet it. It flows from the Holy Spirit (Galatians 5:22). He will fulfil, by his power, every desire in us for goodness. This is a crucial promise found in 2 Thessalonians 1:11. Take hold of it as you pray in faith. You belong to Jesus and so you are capable, in a gradually increasing way, of letting your life be "a rich harvest of every kind of goodness" (Ephesians 5:9, GNB). The world needs your life to be like that.

Faithfulness

Some translations of the Bible say simply "faith" or "fidelity" here. The *Jerusalem Bible* has "trustfulness" and this gets close to the core idea of reliability and trustworthiness that is found in this fruit of the Spirit.

Someone said that God does not require brilliance or success, but simply our faithfulness. How reassuring to understand this. This insight helped me a lot in my younger years and still does today.

Like all the fruit we are considering, faithfulness springs from God. "The Lord is faithful," declares Paul in 2 Thessalonians 3:3. Specifically, he is faithful "to strengthen you and keep you safe from the evil one." This is underlined in Hebrews 2:17-18 where Jesus is described as faithful and able to help those who are tempted. So faithfulness in you consists of the Holy Spirit helping to make and keep you consistent in your faith and in your Christian service. No stopping and starting all the time. No letting others down by inconsistency. Faithfulness, in the sense of loyalty, becomes a key requirement if a position of leadership or responsibility in the congregation is to come your way. "It is required that those who have been given a trust must prove faithful" (1 Corinthians 4:2). Read Revelation 2:10 and note the prize that is at stake for being faithful to the Lord. My prayer is that one day this prize will be yours.

Meekness

Never fall into the trap of mistaking meekness for weakness. The NIV says "gentleness." In the GNB you will find "humility" used instead of "meekness," but meekness is exactly the right word. A meek person is not a weak person. Moses was "meek" (Numbers 12:3, GNB), more meek than anyone else alive according to the Bible, yet he was one of the greatest figures in the Old Testament! The NIV describes him as "a very humble man." Again, we ought not to confuse humility with weakness.

If you pray to be clothed with meekness you are asking God to make you teachable. It has nothing to do with being timid!

There are some memorable promises in Scripture for the meek. Psalm 37:11 has them inheriting the earth, and Jesus repeated this (Matthew 5:5) as though to reinforce it. Psalm 149:4 says the Lord will honor (AV: "beautify") the meek. So it would appear there is some point to this meekness thing after all!

Jesus spoke of his own meekness when he invited men and women to come to him if they were heavily burdened. Out of his meekness he offered, and still offers, rest (Matthew 11:28, 29). "I am gentle and humble (meek) in heart," he said. In other words, he is not high and mighty in spirit. I wonder if this would be a good definition of being meek, not being high and mighty in spirit. It may be of use to you to think of it in this way, especially as you pray about this fruit in your own life and attitudes. Your maturing into real meekness will save you from ever thinking you know best all the time or that there is nothing you can be taught. The absence of meekness in a Christian is a very unattractive thing and suggests a measure of spiritual poverty.

One last suggestion about meekness. The Greek word at the root of the concept can mean "soothing," so think of your meekness being used by the Holy Spirit to affect others like a soothing ointment affects a wound or sting. Perhaps we can say that a meek person is one who can take the heat, or sting, out of a situation. I like this idea and am kneeling with you in prayer for more meekness from God for both of us.

Self-control

Self-control for a Christian is really God-control, for we are meant to yield every aspect of ourselves and of our lives to him. But the New Testament's choice is to refer to self-control. It means restraining certain natural impulses: temper, a tendency to laziness, bodily appetites for food, sex, etc., overspending on ourselves, or any form of selfishness. It is not hard to think of other examples. Self-control is the opposite of self-indulgence, or unhealthy over-indulgence. Sometimes it is spoken of as temperance or moderation, not being given to silly or extravagant extremes.

Strangely enough, when Paul the Apostle appeared before Governor Felix at Caesarea, falsely accused of starting a riot, he chose to debate with Felix, among other things, the merits of self-control (Acts 24:25). His broad theme was faith in Jesus Christ (verse 24) and it is noteworthy that he saw "goodness" and "self-control" (verse 25) as being at the heart of the practical results of believing in Jesus. No wonder it was at this point that Felix called the trial proceedings to a halt! Paul's words must have begun to strike home!

Self-control is singled out in the New Testament as especially called for in the following persons (see Titus 1 and 2):

1. Church elders (1:8)
2. Older Christian men (2:2)
3. Younger Christian women (2:5)
4. Younger Christian men (2:6)
5. All Christians! (2:12)

So nobody is left out. Self-control is a normative aspect of Christian living. The self-controlled life is also an "upright" and "godly" life (Titus 2:12). Resist the temptation to think self-control in this sense can be self-induced. It can't. Like all the fruits of the Spirit it is from God. How is it received? How are any of the fruits received? On one's knees. Even a small child knows that if he wants something he should ask for it. You are God's child. Ask. Ask in faith.

Chapter 6

Being before doing

Will God Equip Me to Serve Him?

Fruits and gifts

Please do not read this chapter (or the next) if you have not yet read chapter 5! Stop now! It is a bad idea to focus your interest upon spiritual gifts, often known as "the gifts of the Spirit," unless you have truly begun to see the prior importance of the fruits of the Spirit. More on this in a moment. First let's be sure that some of the terminology we are using is fully understood.

The previous chapter introduced the fruit or fruits of the Spirit, personality-enhancing and character-forming qualities essential for every believer in a steadily increasing measure. In turning now to look at the gifts of the Spirit it may be helpful to notice a couple of words used in New Testament Greek. *Charis* means grace, i.e. God's freely-bestowed favor and goodwill toward us. *Charisma* (plural *charismata*) means something given as a result of grace, in short, a grace-gift or a spiritual gift.

Now in the New Testament, and in particular in the writings of Paul, we find that *charisma* and *charismata* are used in a very broad and general way. Sometimes, for example, Paul refers to specific gifts of the Holy Spirit (e.g. see 1 Corinthians 7:7, "each man has his own gift from God"). But he also uses the expression to refer to God's free gift of salvation through Jesus (Romans 5:15, 16; 6:23). Yet again, he uses the same Greek word sometimes to mean simply a general blessing or encouragement from God (Romans 1:11; 1 Corinthians 1:7).

It is clear, therefore, that *charisma* and *charismata* are not specialized or technical terms for Paul. It is important for you to get hold of this, because you will hear of, and perhaps may meet, Christians who treat these terms as terribly significant. You will hear references to "charismatic Christians" and "charismatic churches." Some people want to describe themselves as "a charismatic." They mean that they think the gifts of the Holy Spirit are immensely important and that they possess and exercise one or more of these, often in public worship.

To use the terminology in this way is, of course, relatively harmless providing it is remembered that it is not the way the Bible uses it. Rightly speaking, every Christian is a charismatic Christian, for two reasons:

1. God's *charisma* (gift) of salvation applies to all believers (Romans 5:15).

2. Every believer is given from God at least one spiritual *charisma* (gift), according to Paul's teaching in 1 Corinthians 12:11.

Before we study the New Testament lists of the gifts, it would be wise to go back now to the word of caution with which this chapter began.

First things first!

Just after my student days I came to know a fellow Christian at my place of work. Peter, who labelled himself as a "charismatic" Christian, was a good witness, never hiding his faith. He was intelligent and reasonably well-informed about his beliefs.

One day I gave him a ride home in my car and as we stopped outside his house he said, "Shaw, I would like to introduce you to the Holy Spirit." Peter knew very well that I was a Christian and I found his words a little strange. He went on to refer to the gifts of the Holy Spirit and especially the gift of speaking in tongues. He was very earnest and sincere. He felt sure I needed this word from him.

I replied that I knew about the gifts of the Spirit and was open to God to receive whatever he might wish to give me. It became obvious, however, that Peter wanted me to speak in tongues. He seemed to think that unless I did so I could not possibly be Spirit-filled. This is what his church had taught him (mistakenly) when he was first saved.

Well, Peter and I went on for many months as good colleagues together and we had lots of conversations about the work of the Holy Spirit in the life of an individual believer. I could find nothing in my Bible about a test of one special gift to tell if a person was alive in the Holy Spirit. I knew that the Spirit had been active in my own acceptance of Christ as Savior and since then had shown me more and more my need for purity and wholeness (holiness) in every aspect of my life and character. I was actively seeking to surrender more of myself to God's loving control and felt he was calling me to serve him in some full-time way, and that he would equip me as time went on.

One day, quite unexpectedly, Peter raised this whole matter again. This time his words indicated a new and deeper understanding. He said, "I've concentrated on the gifts of the Spirit since I was saved, wanting more and more of them. I wish someone had taught me about holiness and purity of life before I had been taught about the gifts. I've been getting the priorities mixed up." Frankly, yes he had. But how humble (meek) of him to admit it in this way.

Peter was not the first to fail to put first things first and he won't be the last. You, however, can know that the fruits of the Spirit are more important than the gifts of the Spirit. The fruits have to do with who you are, what sort of person you are, what your character is. The gifts have to do with service and ministry for God. It makes no sense to ask, "What can I do?" or "How can I serve?" before you ask, "Who am I?" or "What am I like?" In other words, being comes before doing. There is no more certain recipe for disaster than to attempt to exercise spiritual gifts from the basis of an unsanctified life. A Christian who seeks to offer ministry through a spiritual gift or gifts, and yet who lacks meekness of character or who is loveless, will do damage not good, and should refrain.

The gifts of the Spirit are like adornments which we put on our bodies. There is no point or gain in adding adornments to a body which remains in serious respects unclean and impure. So, first in priority is the cleansing and the character-building in the likeness of Christ; then, and only then, the gifts in service to others.

New Testament lists of spiritual gifts

The Scriptures teach that God equips his people to serve him. He does this by the conferring of a spiritual gift or gifts upon each believer. This is the work of the Holy Spirit. He alone determines which gift you will receive. Every Christian has at least one gift (1 Corinthians 12:11). Some have more. The more you get, the more the Lord expects from you. Being greatly gifted by the Holy Spirit is a wonderful thing, but it is an enormous burden of responsibility too. You cannot manipulate God. His will, as in all things, is sovereign. Whatever your gift, receive it with gladness and use it with humility. Thank God for it. Never boast about it.

There are four lists in the New Testament. Before reproducing them below, I want to emphasize that each list is surrounded by repeated references to the need for unity and for *agape* love among believers. It is really important to read the lists in their overall contexts. The early Christian church experienced quarrels and division over which gifts mattered most. That is why the lists appear with a great stress upon unity and love. Therefore, let your personal resolve be, from the start, that you will do your utmost to maintain unity with your fellow believers as you use your gift for God, and that you will never use it for selfish purposes or in a loveless and uncaring manner.

The lists of gifts and their *contexts* are as follows, using the GNB:

1. Ephesians 4:4-16

    Verses 4-6
    "show your *love*"
    "preserve the *unity*"
    "there is *one body* and *one Spirit*"

    Verse 11:
    "He appointed some to be
    - apostles
    - prophets
    - evangelists
    - pastors
    - teachers"

    Verses 12-16:
    "*build up* the body of Christ"
    "*oneness* in our faith"
    "become *mature people*"
    "under his control all the different parts of the body fit together"
    "the whole body grows ... through *love*"

2. Romans 12:4-10

    Verses 4, 5:
    "*one body* ... different functions"
    "we are *one body* in *union* with Christ"
    "we are *all joined* to each other as different parts of *one body*"

Verses 6-8: "our different gifts"
- to speak God's message (prophecy)
- to serve (service)
- to teach (teaching)
- to encourage (encouragement, exhortation)
- to share (sharing, giving)
- to have authority (leadership)
- to show kindness (acts of mercy)

Verses 9, 10:
"*love* must be completely sincere"
"*love* one another warmly"
"show *respect* for one another"

3. 1 Corinthians 12:4-13; ch. 13
Verses 4-7:
"the *same* Spirit"
"the *same* Lord"
"the *same* God"
"for the good of *all*"

Verses 8-10:
"The Spirit gives ..."
- wisdom
- knowledge
- faith
- power to heal
- miracles
- speaking God's message (prophecy)
- telling the difference between gifts (discernment)

- tongues
- explaining what is said in tongues (interpretation)

Verses 11-13:
"Christ is like a *single body*"
"*one body* ... of different parts"
"we have all been given the *one Spirit*"
"if I have no *love,* this does me no good" (13:3)
"faith, hope, and *love;* and the greatest of these is *love*" (13:13)

4. First Corinthians 12:27-14:1
   Verse 27:
   "*all* of you are Christ's body"
   "*each one* is a part of it"

   Verse 28:
   "In the church God has put ..."
   - apostles
   - prophets
   - teachers
   - those who perform miracles
   - those given the power to heal
   - those who help others (helpers)
   - those who direct others (administrators)
   - those who speak in tongues

Ch. 13:1-14:1
"if I have no *love* ..."
"*love* is patient ... kind" etc.

"there are gifts ... but they will cease"
"our gifts ... are only partial"
"the greatest ... is *love*"
"it is *love,* then, that you should strive for"

I hope you have seen clearly the New Testament pattern. All these lists come from the pen of the Apostle Paul. He knew how divisive the wrong use of gifts could be and how much damage could result to individual Christians and to the Church if some envied the gifts of others or, conversely, if some looked down on others. Hence his overriding anxiety to underline time and again the absolutely central place to be given to preserving unity among the believers and treating one another with Christ-like love. These themes are highlighted by the words italicized in the lists and their contexts shown above.

Some comments on the lists:

1. No two lists are identical. It appears that Paul did not have a fixed system in mind. Neither then should we. The Holy Spirit cannot be pinned down to written lists. Although there are 22 separate gifts mentioned, we ought not to imagine the lists are closed. They are illustrative of the main or most commonly received gifts.

2. The order in which the gifts are placed varies from list to list. Notice, however, that speaking in tongues (or interpreting tongues) is invariably placed last (rather like Judas in the lists of disciples) as though to signal its lack of central importance. Speaking in tongues had been elevated beyond reason in Corinth and Paul was eager to play it down (see the next chapter).

3. The lists in 1 Corinthians 12 have to be read and

understood in the context of chapters 12-14. These three chapters are a unit. Chapter 13 is pivotal to Paul's whole concept of spiritual gifts, its theme actually beginning in the last verse of chapter 12. More will be said on this "love chapter" in a moment.

4. Some of the gifts are supernatural, like miracles, healing, prophecy, etc. Others are not at all spectacular and are quite natural, even everyday, such as helping, service and encouragement. The vital point is that it is the same God and the same Holy Spirit who inspires each gift (1 Corinthians 12:6, 11). The more natural gifts may be held and used unconsciously. It is possible to have a gift and not know it by its Bible name. Many Christians are in this position, responding spontaneously and naturally in their daily living to the leadings of God, never for a moment tempted into any of the pitfalls or the pride sometimes associated with the gifts.

5. Prophecy is in all four of the lists and is stressed by Paul to be useful for building up (edifying) other believers (1 Corinthians 14). Teaching spiritual truth is in three of the four lists. See the next chapter for more detailed comment on each of the gifts.

6. The over-arching emphasis which comes across in these New Testament passages is the sovereign control of God. Each gift, all gifts, come from him. Each is apportioned by him according to his sovereign will (1 Corinthians 12:11). Every single Christian has at least one gift which equips for service and which, rightly and lovingly used, contributes its part to the building up of the whole body of Christ on earth, the Church. No Christian is giftless.

7. On the other hand, no single believer can expect to receive all the gifts. All the fruits of the Spirit, yes—to a greater or lesser extent—but not all the gifts (see 1 Corinthians 12:29-31). Neither, according to the sense of these verses, is there one particular gift given to all believers. The claim sometimes heard that tongues is given to all is a false claim and without Scriptural foundation.

No love, no gain

It is worth taking a few moments to look more closely at 1 Corinthians 13. Often it is read alone and thus out of context. Similarly, chapters 12 and 14 are studied without reference to chapter 13 which is, in fact, the principal focus of Paul's entire approach to the matter of spiritual gifts.

Notice first of all that *agape* love can be seen as being both a fruit (see chapter 5) and a gift of the Holy Spirit. Just as it is love which binds all the other fruits together (Colossians 3:14), so love is the gift above all other gifts (1 Corinthians 12:31; 13:13), without which all lesser gifts are useless. Perhaps, rather than regarding love as a separate and distinctive gift, we might see it as an absolutely indispensable element in all the gifts listed in the New Testament, so that instead of speaking about prophecy, for example, we would do better to speak of loving-prophecy, or loving-teaching, or loving-leadership and so on.

So strong is the Bible's emphasis on the indispensability of love in this famous and eloquent passage that we find the word *agape* (love) used 12 times but *charismata* (gifts) only twice. This is the balance to adopt in our own thinking and, indeed, in our own living. *Agape* love is a way of living that relegates to insignificance the claims of this or that particular gift.

No matter how elevated our speaking, and even if we speak like angels, loveless tongues or loveless utterances are as meaningless as a gong swinging in the breeze. Worse than this, it is the speaker himself that is meaningless: "if ... I have not love, I am nothing" (verse 2). Loveless prophecy and loveless faith are just as worthless (verse 2). The same is true for the loveless exercise of less spectacular gifts like giving (verse 3). Even self-sacrifice in martyrdom (not included in the four lists of gifts) is useless if mis-motivated (verse 3).

The *agape* lifestyle (verse 4) manifests patience in the face of suffering and repays with kindness when hurt is received. It does not envy the spiritual gifts of others, nor boast about its own giftedness. It is not proud or arrogant (literally, "puffed up" about itself).

Where *agape* rules (verse 5), you will find no rudeness or ill manners, but instead a proper behavior which causes embarrassment to none. Neither will you find worship of self, but instead a refusal to trample on the rights of others and a willingness to let go what is rightfully held. Neither is *agape* easily wound-up, touchy or hiding a foul temper just below a seemingly tranquil surface. The presence of *agape* leaves no room for a secret catalog of grudges. This is baggage that must go if we are to walk at Christ's pace.

Christlike love (verse 6) does not take pleasure in the wrongs done by others or secretly rejoice in the knowledge of others' weaknesses. It shuns salaciousness or impropriety, even in secret. It openly joins with others in celebrating righteousness and purity of life. It rejoices in truth. It is persistent, enduring, trustworthy, hopeful and persevering (verse 7).

If there is a test of the active presence of the Holy Spirit in a believer, then evidence of *agape* love must satisfy that test. After all, the gifts can be faked. In New Testament times the rituals of pagan worship included manifestations similar in appearance and effect to those of certain of the spiritual gifts known in Christian circles. That is why we are told to "test" those who claim to have the Holy Spirit (see 1 John 4:1-3), to see if their gift is from God or from the Enemy of Christ ("antichrist"). That is also why reference is made to the gift of discernment or the ability to tell the difference between gifts that come from the Spirit and those that do not (1 Corinthians 12:10). Put another way, it is much more impressive and convincing to see love grow in a person where none grew before and to see other fruit of the Spirit blossom where before nothing bloomed. No person can do this for himself. For evidence of a Spirit-filled life we look for the fruits, not the gifts.

For completeness, the next chapter will consider in a little more detail some selected gifts of the Spirit. Please do not read it unless you have first spent time in chapter 5 and then in this present chapter. The comments on individual gifts are intended merely to be adequate to answer most of the basic questions likely to arise in the mind of a relatively new Christian.

(Please note that the gift of evangelism is considered briefly in chapter 10 and not in the next chapter.)

CHAPTER 7

Some brief explanations

What Are the Gifts of the Spirit?

If you are dipping into this book at random or even in search of specific topics, please do not read this chapter unless you have first read chapter 5 which is about Christlikeness of character, the primary need of all Christians whether new or experienced. You need also to read chapter 6 before going on, in order to grasp the relationship between the fruit and the gifts of the Holy Spirit. This is essential background to what now follows.

Apostles

The Greek word *apostolos* means "one who is sent." The apostles were thus those sent by God to do his will in the world, proclaim his salvation and to found his Church. Normally we use this expression to refer to the 12 disciples of Jesus plus Paul (on Paul see Romans 1:5). In

1 Corinthians 15:7 it refers to the Twelve, minus Judas. There are a few New Testament examples of the word being applied more widely than just to the Twelve and Paul: Philippians 2:25 (to Epaphroditus), Romans 16:7 (to Andronicus and Junias) and 2 Corinthians 11:13 (to "false apostles").

When Paul states in 1 Corinthians 12:28 that apostles have been placed "first" in the church by God he means not only first in importance but also first in order of time. Historically they came before Christian prophets and teachers. It follows that the status or role of an apostle is confined to that historical period. There are no more apostles, in the scriptural sense, appointed since New Testament times.

Prophets

Prophecy is for building up other believers through help, encouragement and comfort (1 Corinthians 14:3). The Old Testament prophets were spokespersons for God and carried enormous spiritual authority. They declared God's messages for the here and now and also pointed forward to future events. Their function comprised both forthtelling (proclamation) and foretelling (prediction). Once we get into the Christian era we notice that the status of prophets changes. The real successors of the Old Testament prophets were not the New Testament Christians who were given the gift of prophecy, but the apostles. Once duly recognized as a prophet, the utterances of an Old Testament prophet would not be challenged. They might be ignored, but never were they alleged to be uninspired by God.

Contrast this with the New Testament situation where the words of a prophet are to be "judged" (GNB) or "weighed" (NIV) (1 Corinthians 14:29) and where the authority of an apostle exceeds that of one with the gift of prophecy (verses 37, 38). Note too how Paul (an apostle) ignores a prophetic warning not to go to Jerusalem (Acts 21:4).

Words spoken in what is thus claimed today to be through a gift of prophecy have to be carefully assessed. They cannot automatically be assumed to be God-inspired. There will be a mix of chaff and wheat. How then can we know which is which? The late David Watson suggested a threefold test to aid discernment as to whether the words were of God or simply made up by the speaker:

1. Does the speaker recognize Jesus as Lord (1 Corinthians 12:3)?

2. Does the speaker recognize Jesus as truly and properly God and also as truly and properly man (1 John 4:2)?

3. Does the speaker's life show real godliness and holiness (Matthew 7:15-20)?

Positive answers to these basic questions will help determine the likelihood of the message being of God or not. Furthermore, if the speaker goes on at inordinate length, hindering others with an inspired word to say, it is unlikely that his words are more than self-inspired (1 Corinthians 14:29, 30).

Notice that speaking in prophecy is controllable by

the speaker (1 Corinthians 14:32). It is not a case of people being taken over by some weird force outside themselves. A prophet is not a robot! The one with a genuine gift of prophecy can choose whether to speak or keep silent. He or she can also decide how much to say and when to sit down!

This brings us naturally to the subject of preaching. There is no general agreement as to whether the expounding of Scripture in preaching should be regarded as prophecy. Professor James Packer has expressed this view: "The essence of prophetic ministry was forthtelling God's present word to his people and this regularly meant application of revealed truth rather than augmentation of it ... Any verbal enforcement of biblical teaching as it applies to one's present hearers may properly be called prophecy today, for that in truth is what it is." I am not entirely convinced that Professor Packer is right to include all expository preaching within his definition of prophecy. What I do know, however, is that many a preacher rises to speak and quite without pre-planning finds that the message being delivered is not the one prepared. Or frequently the preacher, with barely a premeditated thought, will feel compelled to depart from what has been prepared and speak words directly from the heart or spirit within. This may be for seconds or minutes only. Almost invariably such words will strike home to one of the listeners. Sometimes that listener will say so to the preacher when leaving at the end of the meeting.

If you are given the gift of prophecy it is unlikely to come to you upon the basis of an immature experience of God. It is one of the higher gifts (not the highest, for that is Christlike love) and you are free to pray for it (1 Corinthians 12:31; 14:1). Messages will not come to you in some ecstatic or pre-packed form. It is the ideas in the prophecy that are inspired, not the words themselves. We know this because prophecies today are spoken in the language and vocabulary of the recipient. A highly educated person will use a vocabulary different from someone of another educational background for delivering the same message. Beware of anyone claiming his or her words are inspired verbatim. This is something we do not even claim for the various translations of the Scriptures!

Teachers

The gift of teaching should not trigger images of schools and classrooms! If you have had a negative experience of school or college do not let that prejudice you against this gift. It is a beautiful gift which God uses to increase and deepen understanding of the faith and of God's ways on the part of believers.

Teachers, in this New Testament sense, are mature Christians who are empowered by God, through the Holy Spirit, to instruct and teach others in matters of belief. Thus the basics, and also the finer points, of the Christian faith are made intelligible.

The gift can be exercised in various settings: on a one-to-one basis; in a lecture; in a Bible study group; in a sermon; in a Sunday school room and so on. It can also be exercised through the written word, such as in letters, lecture notes, or in books, pamphlets and articles.

Tongues and their interpretation

This gift is included in this chapter, not because it is one of the higher gifts (for it is not) but because it has aroused and still arouses puzzlement and even controversy. It need not do so, provided the teaching of the Scriptures is understood and adhered to.

Tongues in the New Testament era consisted of two separate phenomena. The first is speaking in a language which the speaker has never learned. The speaker does not at all understand what is being said. Known technically as *xenoglossia* (pronounced as though starting with a "z"), this appears to be what happened by the power of God in Acts chapter 2 on the Day of Pentecost: "All of them were filled with the Holy Spirit and began to speak in other languages." Verse 6 records that a large crowd gathered and "each one heard them speaking in his own language." Verses 7-11 repeatedly underline this fact.

The second form of speaking in tongues is known as *glossolalia*. This is speaking in verbal patterns that cannot be identified with any human language. Again the speaker is ignorant of the meaning of the sounds uttered. Paul describes this as praying with one's spirit but not with one's mind (1 Corinthians 14:14) and pointedly goes on at once to extol the virtues of involving the mind (verses 15-19). Paul was greatly gifted in tongues-speaking (verse 18) but insists that in public worship he would rather speak just five words that could be understood by himself and others than 10,000 in a tongue, because this would "instruct others" (verse 19). Notice the criterion for using this gift—whether or not it will help others and build them up in the faith. Paul uses the same test for ranking the gifts, especially for ranking tongues in relation to prophecy. Read verses 1-5. On this test, tongues is given the lowest place.

As with prophecy, tongues is controllable by the speaker. Paul tells the Christians in Corinth not to speak in tongues in public worship if no one with a gift of interpretation is present (verse 28). Regrettably, this Scriptural guideline is often ignored in modern congregations where sometimes the leader invites the whole company to speak or sing aloud in tongues. There is no Scriptural warrant for this mass use of tongues. It is a practice which makes the unbeliever feel excluded (14:16) and which wrongly, even unlovingly, assumes that everyone has the same gift, again an assumption without a Scriptural basis (12:29, 30).

The twentieth century experience of tongues has been shown by research to be *glossolalia* rather than *xenoglossia*. The sounds produced reflect the user's native tongue and even regional accents. The gift would seem to be best used, and frequently is so used to great benefit, in private and solitary prayer. Paul all but rules it out in public worship (verse 19). He had previously visited Corinth "with a demonstration of the Spirit's power" (2:4). This may have involved his exercising various spiritual gifts, perhaps including tongues. At any rate, tongues had been elevated to an undeserved place in the life of the Corinthian church, necessitating Paul's detailed consideration of it in 1 Corinthians 14. There he restores the right emphasis—the higher gifts are those that edify and encourage others and which build up the church: "Let all things (i.e. when you come together) be done for edification" (verse 26, RSV). Since "he who speaks in a tongue edifies *himself*" (verse 4), the practice has no place in public worship unless the tongues-speaker knows that someone gifted in interpretation is present (verse 28).

Notice that this latter gift is not a gift of translation, but of interpretation. The interpreter does not understand the sounds uttered any more than the tongues-user. The concepts and ideas in the message are made intelligible by the Holy Spirit to the interpreter as the tongues are spoken or when they stop.

Beware of taking up some extreme attitude toward tongues. Do not be dismissive of it. Do not fear it, but do not envy it either. It is not for every Christian and is, in any case, a low-ranking gift. Ask God for the higher gifts. Those who use tongues in their private prayers enjoy thereby a sense of wellbeing and are personally helped. Not everyone, however, needs this in order to be close to God in prayer. Like all spiritual gifts, tongues is a beautiful thing when rightly used. The history of the early Church and of the twentieth century Church shows, sadly, that when it is abused, or wrongly insisted upon as some sort of proof of spiritual status, it is highly damaging to the body of Christ.

Faith

The gift of faith does not encompass saving faith, the faith a person puts in Jesus as Savior in order to become a Christian in the first place. All Christians know saving faith. The gift of the Spirit known as faith is the implanting by the Holy Spirit in the heart of a believer such an exceptional measure of faith, belief and trust in the power of God that great works for God and his Kingdom are brought to pass as a result. This is the faith that moves mountains, to use a Scriptural metaphor (Mark 11:22, 23).

Hebrews 11 is a famous New Testament chapter dealing with faith and listing great people of faith who trusted God in a special way long before Jesus was born. They laughed at impossibilities! As the old gospel chorus says: "God specializes in things thought impossible!"

There are modern examples of faith too. George Muller of Bristol, England, comes readily to mind. He worked among homeless children but lived by faith, simply telling God his needs for money. Money came, always just enough for God's work to be achieved.

Occasionally you may come across fellow Christians who are said to be "living by faith." That is to say, they are entirely at God's full-time disposal, have no secular means of support and are quietly, even secretly, relying on God to supply their material needs. Often such people have a gift of faith. Be wary, however, of any who actually announces to you that they are living by faith. That gives the game away and is a thinly disguised form of begging!

Healings

I recommend to you David Watson's poignant book on this subject. Entitled *Fear No Evil* and published in the USA in 1985 by Shaw publications, it airs all the relevant issues in a most helpful and practical way. Watson rightly believed that God could heal miraculously and was himself the recipient of healing ministry but which did not save his life. His book answers many valid questions and the author's personal circumstances give it both authority and sensitivity.

Notice that in the original Greek of 1 Corinthians 12:9, 28, 29 this gift is consistently referred to in the plural, not the singular. The word used is "healings" or "cures." We are therefore dealing with a gift of healings or a gift of cures. This suggests a gift given to be used on special occasions only. It may even be a gift given by God only on one occasion for one person's ailment. The pattern may vary and we should not assume that because God has used us once or twice we need to launch out on a public healing ministry!

Praying for healing for others is always appropriate. Realize, however, that sometimes the answer will be "no." If led to pray for someone's physical healing, pray just as earnestly that they will know the grace of God to bear the illness or infirmity with Christlike fortitude and that their faith will not fail. Remember Paul's "thorn in the flesh" (GNB: "a painful physical ailment"—2 Corinthians 12:7). Three times Paul asked God to heal him, but God answered with a "no." His answer was: "My grace is sufficient for you, for my power is made perfect in weakness" (2 Corinthians 12:9). Paul's reaction, in the end, was: "I delight in weaknesses ..." (verse 10). He was ready to recognize that God may have had a higher purpose in withholding healing. God's purposes are good and sure, even if we cannot see them yet.

Helping

This is probably the most widely bestowed spiritual gift and therefore one that is crucial to the building-up of the Church, the body of Christ. It is greatly undervalued and often goes unrecognized both by those exercising it and by others.

It takes an infinite variety of forms. Its essence is an ongoing and marked willingness to be at God's disposal for relatively routine and generally unsung tasks. Those receiving the gift are often ready to roll up their sleeves and get their hands dirty. I have witnessed this gift in Christians cleaning and sweeping, helping to sort old clothes, providing transportation, picking up hymnals, baking cakes, shopping, arranging flowers, fundraising, painting and decorating—the list is endless!

The gift includes not only a remarkable spirit of willingness to serve God in these ordinary but vital ways, but also a capacity to see and identify the need for a job to be done. Oh, for more believers like this!

Administration

It is often mistakenly thought that the gift of administration has to do with administration in the sense used in the world of business. I have met Christians, even Christian leaders, who claim to have this gift because they are good at running an office, or doing paperwork, or are generally adept at organizing Christian events, etc. All of this comes closer to the gift of helping than of administration.

The various translations of the Bible offer different words: GNB has "directing"; RSV has "administrators";

KJV has "gifts of governments." The Greek word in the original text is *kyberneseis,* which literally means "navigation." We get our modern English word "cybernetics" from it. To get closer to the heart of this gift it is helpful to focus on the concept of navigating a ship. Think of getting a vessel from place A to place B on time and by the right route. Then think of a church or a diocese or a Salvation Army corps or division, even a whole territory, and the need to navigate it from where it is today in its life, ministry and witness to where God wants it to be at some future date in terms of its effectiveness. To accomplish this the Holy Spirit confers upon some Christian leaders a gift, as it were, of navigation in spiritual things. It involves constant waiting on the Lord for guidance, a willingness to trust him and a readiness to gauge by his help when, or when not, to take risks for God.

Discovering your gifts

There is a trend today for questionnaires which are designed to help you discover which gift or gifts of the Spirit have been given to you. I sometimes wonder how we ever managed to know what God was up to before these questionnaires hit the market!

It takes time to realize what abilities God is placing within you. Remember that you have natural talents which will be enormously enhanced when used for God's purposes and the benefit of others. In addition, the Holy Spirit will gift you supernaturally with at least one spiritual gift. Be patient. Remain open. Stay humble.

Do not rush to conclude that a particular gift is

yours. Allow yourself time and opportunity to realize with a steadily growing conviction that God has granted you something specific. Doors will open to you presenting situations in which you can be of service and calling for some ability or another. Take these opportunities and assess your progress for yourself. Did it go well? Did you feel at ease? How costly to you in nervous energy was the experience? Did anyone seem helped? Has anyone told you they were helped or encouraged by what you did or said? A sensible and prayerful consideration of questions like these will help you to know the direction in which the Lord is working in you. You would be wise also, once you have been able to experiment a bit, to talk things over with a mature Christian friend or leader.

Later years may bring a discovery of still further gifts and abilities. The Lord is always ready to surprise us and to do a new thing! He is also ready to remove from us that which has been received from him but which has been selfishly used, for example, for personal glory or boasting. That is why, once we know the gift he has bestowed, we ought never to cease to thank him for it and to plead with him for grace to use it properly and in a spirit of Christlike love.

CHAPTER 8

Holiness now!

Will I Ever Be A Saint?

The problem of your future sins
Not long ago I asked a group of Christians: "Which of you stopped sinning from the moment you were saved?" Not one wished to make this claim. All acknowledged that their conversions to Christ had not resulted in an end to sinning, although they were sure they were saved.

Before becoming Christians they had, like everyone else, been under sin and not holy in any sense at all. As William Booth once said, an unsaved person is totally unholy "from the crown of his head to the sole of his foot!" Realizing they could not free themselves from sin, the members of the group had, in their own time, found Jesus as Savior. They ceased to be under sin. Instead they were under grace, or to put it another way, were now over sin. They were no longer in rebellion toward God and had sought and found forgiveness for past sins. However, and this is the heart of the matter, each had found that the old sins of pride and temper, or whatever, still existed within. The sins could still rise up and were not dead! Past yielding to them was forgiven in Jesus, yes, but the old sins still proved troublesome. They were bruised and weakened maybe, but undoubtedly still alive.

Before conversion this did not cause unease, or a troubling of conscience, at least not until the first longings for something better. Now, however, with a knowledge of the Lord and having caught sight of and tasted his purity, the nagging and persistence of the old sins were a source of decided spiritual discomfort. The new Christians were simply not satisfied with continuing to fall into sin. They knew they could repent sincerely and begin again, but something seemed to say to them that things did not have to go on like this. Surely, there had to be something better than a ceaseless cycle of falling and repenting, falling and repenting.

They longed for the power of sin to be broken in their lives, having known the joy and relief when the guilt of their past sins had been canceled by the grace of God as they first trusted in Jesus to save them. After all, what did it mean in Charles Wesley's great hymn when it said of Jesus: "He breaks the power of canceled sin?" And what did the Scriptures mean when they spoke of God's promise to his people to make them clean and give them a new heart, a new spirit and to save them from everything that defiled them (Ezekiel 36:26-29)? Could not God make believers holy in every way and keep their whole spirit, soul and body "blameless" (1 Thessalonians 5:23)?

These feelings have been present in Christian believers from the birth of the Church. The longing for a truly pure and holy life in full and unconditional obedience to God is not new. Already, since your own conversion, it may have sprung up in your heart. I hope that it has. May I address to you gently the same question that was mentioned at the start of this chapter? Have you found that you have continued to fall into sin since you first came to Christ for forgiveness?

If so, what do you propose to do about it? Are you seeking a remedy? Do you share a longing for holiness and wholeness of life? This is what I mean by the problem of your future sins. To use the words of Frederick Coutts, you are experiencing "the discontent of the forgiven soul." This is not altogether a bad thing.

Holy discontent

Feeling discontent is far better than complacency and thinking you have arrived spiritually. It is prompted within you by the Holy Spirit and, although it can be directly addressed and satisfied, there is a sense in which it will never quite go away. It is God's way of nudging us onward and upward toward more of what he has for us—a deeper likeness to Christ, a greater share in the fruits of the Spirit, a more perfect obedience to his will.

Earlier, in chapter 5, we looked at the fruits of the Spirit, noting carefully the need to be open to the Holy Spirit as these are offered to us in bud form at first and then in increasing measure, until in maturity they bloom in our lives to make us like Christ. All of this has to do directly with moving ahead after accepting Jesus as Savior so that we do not slip back. The more the Holy Spirit is allowed to do his work in us, the less room there is for falling back into sin. The need to move on in this way and to make Christ truly Lord of every facet of our lives has given rise to what is known as the doctrine of holiness. This chapter is designed to be a short introduction to holiness teaching and thus an encouragement to you to go deeper into the things of Christ.

Why a doctrine of holiness?

Well, why a doctrine of anything? The word "doctrine" simply means "teaching."

Matters of faith and belief need to be taught and communicated in words. This need is obvious. Christian doctrine in general is everything that Christians believe about God, the world, salvation, Heaven, Jesus, the holy life and so on. There is a need to formulate our beliefs in a reasonably systematic way so that they can be stated clearly for the purpose of witnessing and sharing our faith, and also for the purpose of teaching them. Doctrine also allows Christians to reach a measure of agreement on matters of belief, thereby keeping false belief and false teaching at bay. Doctrinal formulas are not fences to keep truth locked in, but boundary lines to mark the divide between truth and heresy.

Holiness teaching seeks to reflect the Scriptural material which exhorts us to reach out after the spiritual heights and to live a life that is clean in thought, word and deed. Let's take it in as logical a way as we can, remembering that this chapter is but an introduction.

Flawed, but holy by status

The New Testament regularly refers to the Christians in the early church as "the holy ones." This is the literal translation of the Greek expression *hoi hagioi* which crops up no fewer than 55 times in the New Testament letters. Some Bible versions (e.g. KJV) translate this using the English word "saints." GNB says "God's people," but this does not quite capture the flavor of the original. RSV and NIV, like KJV, use "saints." How interesting that all Christians—good, bad and indifferent—were regarded as saints, as holy ones!

Clearly they could not have been like the canonized saints of the Roman Catholic Church, spiritual giants, some of whom are mentioned earlier in chapter 4. We know for a fact that the first generations of Christian believers were a pretty mixed bunch and did not get things right all the time because there is not a single letter in the New Testament that does not contain rebuke. Yet they are addressed and thought of as saints, literally "the holy ones!" (For instances of this see Romans 1:7; Ephesians 1:1; Philippians 1:1 in the KJV, RSV or NIV. Bible references for the rest of this chapter will be from RSV unless otherwise stated.)

If their lives were flawed and if they were still falling into sin even though they were Christian believers, in what sense could they be called "holy?" The beginnings of an answer to this lies in a grasp of what the people of the Old Testament understood about holiness. They knew the Lord to be holy (Isaiah 6:1). Religious rituals, places, objects, seasons and even persons (such as priests) which were especially associated with the worship of the Lord also came, therefore, to be seen as holy, in the sense of being set aside for God's use and God's purposes. These places, objects and people took on a holy status.

When Paul, in the New Testament, calls the flawed Christians "holy ones" he has this concept in mind. Because they are Christ's followers, they have been called out to be God's holy people, set aside from the world and from unbelievers for the holy purposes of God.

In this way they were holy by status. Their holy status did not always carry over into actual results. It was one thing to be holy in name or by status, but another for their lives to be holy by results. This is just as true for modern Christians. As soon as you were saved you belonged to Christ. You became holy by status in the same sense that Paul says the far-from-perfect recipients of his letters were holy. For most Christians the gap between holy status and holy living is at first a very wide one. Growing in grace and in spiritual maturity is about closing that gap, steadily but surely.

Closing the gap

It is God's sacred will that your living—your thoughts, words, and deeds—should match your status of being someone set aside for his sacred purposes and work. He wants your new standing in Christ to evidence itself in real results and to bear a wonderful harvest of the fruits of the Spirit and of obedience to God. The exhortation of Hebrews 12:1 (NIV) is that we "throw off everything that hinders and the sin that so easily entangles." Verses 10 and 11 of the same chapter tell us that the Lord will apply his loving discipline to us as his children "that we may share in *his* holiness" and produce in our practical living "a harvest of righteousness."

God does not toy with his children. He does not tease us. He does not hold out to us the possibility of practical holy living (*every* sin laid aside) only to snatch it back the moment we take him at his word. If God says he requires it, you can then be positive of two things: a) it is possible; b) he will live in you and work in you by his Holy Spirit to bring it about, if you let him.

Closing the gap between holy status and holy results in everyday living above sin takes time. The gap is not bridged in five minutes any more than Rome was built in a day! We are therefore dealing with an ongoing process which in New Testament Greek is denoted by the word *hagiasmos,* often rendered in English by words like "consecration" or "sanctification." The GNB, in 1 Corinthians 1:30, translates it by the phrase: "we become God's holy people." This captures and conveys the process idea quite well. The process of *hagiasmos* (being made holy) produces in believers *hagiosune* (holiness), even though the believers have been *hoi hagioi* (the holy ones) from when they were first saved. It is a process of moving from mere status (theory) to solid results (practice).

At the same time it is of vital importance to recognize that every process has a starting point. The process of walking to the end of the street starts with the first step. The process of performing a symphony starts with the first note. It is no use having the status of being an orchestra member if you never lift the instrument and make music, although tentatively at first! To use another example, if I wish to be a lawyer I need to qualify. On the day I qualify I am a lawyer by status and nobody can deny it. Yet it is going to take time to complete the process of becoming a mature and experienced lawyer. When I embark on my first case, that process has begun.

So it is that the process of becoming holy must have a starting point. You say, "But it started when I was saved." That is true. Nevertheless, it has been, and is, the experience of the vast majority of Christians that their express and conscious desire to make a clearcut, definite start toward the holy life has arisen subsequent to being saved. So widespread has this been that some have called this a "second blessing." That is nothing but a convenient term for recognizing that most Christians seem to need time, after being saved, to realize just how far-reaching a thing their new commitment is. Those who speak of a "second blessing," therefore, do not mean to imply that what God did for them when they were saved was somehow inadequate and in need of enhancement. They simply use the phrase as a natural way to express their sudden post-conversion awakening to the lovely possibilities for pure living and ongoing victory over temptation that Jesus offers us. Moreover, there is nothing in Scripture which rules out the possibility of new converts seeing all at once, and from the beginning, the whole of what God can do for them. Experience, however, suggests this is rare. Like the disciples of old, most of us are slow to comprehend.

I do want to underline the usefulness of thinking in terms of making a definite start in producing holy results in your living and not settling for being holy by status alone or only in name. As you read more widely you may find that this starting out, this taking of the first step in faith that God can and will keep you pure and free from sin, is sometimes referred to as a "crisis." Be aware of the debate in some circles as to whether this (most usually) "second blessing" should rightly be understood as a process over time or as a crisis, received and settled in one decisive moment. Here "crisis" is used to mean simply a turning point or a watershed moment in one's spiritual experience. The word is not intended to carry any sense of drama or trouble, calamity or panic. This chapter offers the view that it is both a process and a crisis, on the simple ground that every process must have a moment when it is begun. There is, in fact, little to debate.

Breaking sin's hold

All the great teachers and preachers of holiness have recognized that while our conversion to Christ frees us from the guilt of past sin there is a need for believers to trust God to keep them saved and make them pure. No longer under sin, wrongdoing and sinful choices nevertheless still seem to have a definite, though weakened, hold. We considered this at the outset of this chapter. Holiness is about ending sin's hold once and for all, unwinding one by one sin's evil tentacles which hold us back and saying that they shall touch us no more! Martin Luther, John Calvin, John Wesley, William Booth, Catherine Booth, Samuel Brengle—these and others taught and preached that this was a real and practical possibility.

Long ago it was thought that to be truly holy and live above sin you had to turn your back on the world and enter a monastery or a convent. The religious Reformation in Europe in the 1500s saw a new outlook. Martin Luther and John Calvin led the way in promoting the possibility of living a life wholly pleasing to God in the secular world. The great John Wesley travelled England on horseback in the 1700s with the same marvelous message and the outcome was the Evangelical Revival which swept England, revitalizing the churches and transforming communities. William and Catherine Booth enshrined holiness teaching in the formal doctrines of The Salvation Army, with Samuel Logan Brengle becoming the Army's most eloquent writer and exponent of the doctrine. Brengle's books, written over 50 years ago, are still in print and pulsate with challenge even today.

Put quite simply, holiness is Christ. Christ in you. Christ in me. We can never divorce holiness from likeness to Christ. To put it more explicitly, in terms of human attainment the goal of holiness is a life free from all deliberate sinning. Stated so starkly, it immediately seems impossible. To limited human powers, it is. Bring God into it, and the possibilities are limitless! Wait, then, to hear what God says in his word:

Strive ... for the holiness without which no one will see the Lord (Hebrews 12:14).

By a single offering he (Jesus) has perfected for all time those who are sanctified (Hebrews 10:14).

May the Lord make you increase and abound in love ... so that he may establish your hearts unblamable in holiness (1 Thessalonians 3:12, 13).

God has not called us for uncleanness, but in holiness (1 Thessalonians 4:7).

For you have died, and your life is hid with Christ in God ... Put to death therefore what is earthly in you: immorality, impurity ... Put on then, as God's chosen ones, holy and beloved, compassion, kindness, lowliness, meekness and patience (Colossians 3:3-12).

The blood of Jesus Christ ... cleanses us from all sin (1 John 1:7).

Everyone who thus hopes in him purifies himself as he (Jesus) is pure (1 John 3:3).

We know that any one born of God does not sin, but He who was born of God (Jesus) keeps him, and the evil one does not touch him (1 John 5:18).

Now to him who is able to keep you from falling and to present you without blemish ... be glory, majesty, dominion and authority (Jude 24, 25).

In these words from Scripture we can discern not only the beautifully challenging standard God holds out before us, but also his loving, gracious readiness to do within us all that is needed to bring it to pass. There is no need to be deterred. It was Duncan Campbell who said, "Holiness is not human life brought up to the highest level of development, but divine life brought down to the lowest level of condescension."

Do not settle for letting any poisonous trace of sin go unconfronted. The Lord stands with you in "your struggle against sin" (Hebrews 12:4). The entire 12th chapter of Hebrews concentrates upon the call to holiness. Its opening exhortation is that we "lay aside every weight, and sin which clings so closely" so that we can run the race Jesus sets for us. Verse 14 repeats the call to strive for holiness, and is followed by a warning against letting the weeds of sin, which bear poisonous and bitter fruit, have room to grow. Verse 15 relies for its imagery (see RSV's "root of bitterness," NIV's "no bitter root," GNB's "a bitter plant") on an Old Testament passage found in Deuteronomy 29. There Moses spells out again the wishes of the Lord for the Israelites to be his people and for him to be their God (verse 13). They are meant to be a separate people, set aside from other nations for God's will and purpose. That is to say, they were to be a holy people. Therefore Moses warns them against devoting themselves to idols of wood or stone, or even of silver and gold (verse 17). Then he warns them still further of the dire dangers to them and to the others in their community of trying to face in two directions at once, outwardly belonging to the Israelite community but secretly and inwardly turning to false idols. Such persons would be "a root bearing poisonous and bitter fruit" (verse 18).

The writer to the Hebrews picks up this idea and uses it in 12:15 to warn against Christians trying to have a foot in both camps. You cannot belong to the Lord and go on holding close some secret idol or some sinful, poisonous pleasure. Once we are Christ's we are called to single-mindedness. To change the metaphor, we can run his race in one direction only. There are no rewards for dropping out or for running in the wrong direction. That way leads to chaos! Spiritual chaos has a bitter taste.

The pragmatism of holy living

It was Evelyn Underhill, writing in the 1930s but

with lasting relevance, who said, "There is nothing high-minded about Christian holiness. It is most at home in the slum, the street, the hospital ward." It is for the every day, hour by hour. It is for the workplace and the shopping center. It is for our dealings with all manner of people. Most of all, and often most testingly of all, it is for our homelife. None can overestimate the value to God's kingdom of a holy life lived out among one's relatives, especially when those relatives are unsaved and perhaps even skeptical about the gospel. There is no effective argument against the silent eloquence of holiness. Remember the maid who was saved. Her simple yet powerful way of being holy meant that now she swept up everything instead of some of it going under the carpet! Holiness in the everyday!

So many people have a mistaken notion of what holiness involves. They seem to think it's about pious conversation in serious voices! Far from it! Laughter abounds and a sense of humor is essential! A natural, healthy interest in the opposite sex is only to be expected, but lust is out and so too are all forms of sexual impurity. Holiness also sharpens your mind and your opinions. You can speak your mind, but strife, self-indulgent anger, or deliberately cutting words have gone. Irritability as a mark of personality cannot co-exist with the fruits of the Spirit, but natural tension and stress through tiredness are not sins. The believer who has set out for holiness still needs to eat, but is no glutton. He still needs to sleep, but is not addicted to laziness or indolence. He still needs to earn and spend, but is not in love with money. He will want to dress appropriately and will know the latest fashion, but undue pride in personal appearance or lack of modesty will have no place.

Holiness is not exemption from temptation. It is not moral perfection or infallibility. Mistakes will still abound. Holiness does not make a man or woman all-seeing or all-knowing. Neither does it alter our finiteness. Hence the need to recognize that the holy life can still encompass error, and that our errors can still hurt others. In the holy life, "I am sorry, please forgive me" will be words frequently spoken and readily upon the lips.

The essence of holiness is that deliberately choosing to sin has stopped by the rich grace of God. No choosing to lie, to cheat, to defraud, to belittle, to discourage, to slander, to gossip. I like what Bramwell Tripp wrote once. He summed up the possibility of pragmatic holiness in three pithy sentences:

1. To say "I must sin" is to deny my Savior.
2. To say "I cannot sin" is to deceive myself.
3. To say "I need not sin" is to declare my faith in divine power!

Asking God to make you holy

Part of taking a first step, a definite start in the holy life, is to talk to God about it. Here are words set in verse which may be useful to you. They are by Ruth Tracy. They have echoed in many hearts since they were written because they reflect the experience of longing to be good and pure that so many who come to Christ still feel even though they are saved. As I set them down, I pray them again for myself, and sense my spirit's pulse quicken as I think afresh of how much the Lord can do for me.

Will I Ever Be A Saint?

Lord, I come to thee beseeching
For a heart-renewing here;
Unto thee my hands are stretching,
After thee my heart is reaching;
Savior, in thy power draw near.

Holy Spirit, come revealing
All I must forsake, confess;
'Tis for light, Lord, I'm appealing;
I am here to seek thy healing,
Thou art here to save and bless.

'Neath the searching light of Heaven,
Here a deeper truth I see;
Though the past was long forgiven,
One more chain must yet be riven,
Lord, from self I am not free.

Though thy light some pain is bringing,
Thou art answering my prayer;
To thy promises I'm clinging.
At thy cross myself I'm flinging,
For the blood is flowing there.

'Tis the blood, O wondrous river,
Now its power has touched my soul!
'Tis the blood from sin can sever,
'Tis the blood that doth deliver,
Here and now it makes me whole.

We move next to the question of a Christian and money—a real test of the pragmatism of holiness!

CHAPTER 9

Being God's trustee

What About My Money?

We begin with one of the most famous statements in the Bible, and one of the most misquoted too! First Timothy 6:10 does not say that money is the root of all evil, but that "the *love* of money is a root of all kinds of evil." Money itself is a morally neutral thing. It is our attitude to it, and what we do or don't do with it, that is either right or wrong.

Here then is the first and overriding money principle for Christians: do not love money. We do not let it become our master. We do not make it an idol to be worshipped. We do not make it our chief goal in life nor give it a central place. But we are knowledgeable about what it can accomplish, either for good or for ill.

In addition to verse 10, read verses 6-10 and 17-19. These further basic principles will emerge:

    a) learn contentment with what you have;
    b) recognize that you were born poor and will die

poor, for money cannot go beyond this world;
c) be content with an adequacy of basic material possessions such as food and clothing;
d) the quest for wealth is a path littered with pitfalls into which many have fallen, some to their ruin;
e) loving money has even led some to turn their backs on the faith;
f) the rich should recognize that only God, and not money, can ultimately be the ground of their hopes;
g) God is a God of generosity;
h) the rich should use their wealth for good works, sharing generously with others;
i) the godly use of wealth is the only truly safe investment for the future.

These points are worth discussing and I encourage you to find an opportunity to do so, especially with an eye to how they might be applied in real and every day situations, for so often theory is one thing and practice is quite another.

For example, it is easy for me to say at the start of this chapter "do not love money," but what does that mean? Money is at the heart of work, of commerce, even of keeping the Church going in a secular world. Bills have to be paid! So, no idealized pretending that we are free from money. We are not. It touches almost every aspect of life. It was the famous military chaplain, G. A. Studdert Kennedy, a most down-to-earth and honest clergyman, who spelled out that if you love your son or daughter you will want the best that money (or what you have of it) will buy. So love of your child comes face to face with the need for money, and perhaps even the desire for (love of?) it. So does love of knowledge, for knowledge requires books and books cost money. Even love of nature's beauty is not untainted, for the sight of a gorgeous sunset at the coast assumes you can afford to leave town and travel, unless you happen to live by the sea.

Neither is there much honesty in waxing sentimental or idealistic about material poverty. Some, it is true, are called to a life of poverty for the sake of the Lord and service to him. The majority of poor people, however, are poor because of the way society is structured and because of the inequitable and unjust distribution of wealth. For many, poverty is a grinding, debilitating thing. They don't have freedom to dress well, to travel, to receive the best education, to pay for instant medical attention, to plan for a comfortable retirement, or to give something to their children when they die. Recognizing the evil of material poverty is part of Christian realism about money. That is why no Christian worthy of the name will ignore the plight of the poor, whether our Christian response is to the need of an individual "neighbor" (Luke 10:25-37), or to the need to address by social and political action the root causes of poverty. While we shun the love of money, we hate, in the name of Jesus, all that its unjust absence can do to the human body and spirit. At the same time, however, we must not lose sight of the richest truth of all.

Simon's legacy

The greatest, the richest truth of all is that salvation

is offered to everyone free of charge! Long before Jesus came down from glory to walk in full and perfect humanity among us, God's prophet, Isaiah, announced the good news:

> Come, all you who are thirsty, come to the waters; and you who have no money, come, buy and eat! Come, buy wine and milk without money and without cost. Why spend money on what is not bread, and your labor on what does not satisfy? Listen, listen to me, and eat what is good ... Come to me; hear me, that your soul may live.
>
> *(Isaiah 55:1-3)*

God's gift of life is just that—a gift! No money is asked for, none offered is taken. Your soul's eternal destiny cannot be bought and sold in the marketplace. The rich and the poor know ultimate parity in this: all are equal in their need of grace. If anything, it is the rich person who will struggle, for accepting one's need of a Savior means first swallowing one's independence and pride. The poor are more used to dependence. Wasn't it Jesus who, with devastating humor, said something about riches and heaven and camels and needles? Check it out in Mark 10:17-27.

The New Testament has one memorable episode of an attempt to buy spiritual power with money. Acts 8 tells how Peter and John ministered in Samaria and among those who believed their message was Simon, a sorcerer, a performer of magic. When he saw the power of God at work in Peter and John he committed a confused and terrible blunder, offering them money. "Give me also this ability," he said. He thought he could buy a gift of the Spirit! Peter's words to him are recorded for all time: "You have no part or share in this ministry, because your heart is not right before God. Repent of this wickedness ... you are full of bitterness and captive to sin."

Simon's response to these crushingly direct words shows, happily, the beginnings of contrition (verse 24). Nevertheless, to this day Simon's legacy is with us still, for "simony" means the buying and selling of ecclesiastical office for money. Poor Simon learned the hard way that money does not impress God. Empty-handed is the only way to come to him:

> *Nothing in my hand I bring,*
> *Simply to thy cross I cling*

Pulling no punches

If Peter's words to Simon the magician were straight from the shoulder, no less blunt is the teaching of the Epistle of James on the subject of money. The whole letter brims over with practical teaching for Christians and repays intelligent study. Three passages are of immediate relevance.

First, James 1:9-11. This states the principle that our spiritual health should stand apart from, and independent of, our financial status. If you are a poor Christian and you become rich—be glad, says James! If you are a rich Christian and you become poor—also be glad! For gladness of heart is from God, regardless of circumstance. Tough teaching! But the basic fact to remember is that life is fleeting, and riches even more so.

Second, James 2:1-7. In the Simon story of Acts 8 we find that God is unimpressed by wealth. Now in James 2 it is clear that God's people should be similarly unimpressed. The writer uses the illustration of two people coming unexpectedly into your meeting or church service, one obviously rich and one inarguably poor. They are to be given equal courtesy and consideration. No pandering to the wealthy one! No neglecting the lowly one! James reminds us that the gospel came to mankind through plain and humble people—a humble girl, a carpenter, shepherds, fishermen. He goes further and reminds them that the fiercest opponents of the Church at that time were in positions of financial influence.

Third, James 5:1-6. These verses are a ringing condemnation of the selfish and oppressive use of earthly wealth. They are a further underlining of the transitory nature of money: "Your gold and silver are corroded."

James pulls no punches and we, his modern readers, are the better because of it. Others have followed through the centuries, just as forthright, just as trenchant in their proclamation of God's laws. One such person was Catherine Booth (see chapter 4). One of the first women regularly to occupy a pulpit, she became a notable preacher of her day. Speaking in 1881 at the St. James Hall in London, England, one Sunday afternoon, she spelled out the conditions for working successfully for God. Her audience was well-to-do and influential. One of the keys to working successfully for God, she declared, was that you must consecrate your money to God's purposes. What she said that afternoon still rings true: "God never uses anybody largely until they have given up their money. I simply state a fact. We know it so by experience and the history of God's people. You must give up your money ... it must all be given to God, to whom it belongs, being entirely used in his service ... It is a narrow and difficult path ... Consecrate your money and use it to his glory; if you do not, it will eat into your soul as doth a canker." A narrow and difficult path, yes! But Jesus taught that the path that leads to life is such a path (Matthew 7:13, 14)!

Six stimulating chapters

Nobody reading the gospels can sensibly say Jesus did not show an interest in money. He frequently spoke of its effects and its proper use, drawing illustration after illustration from fiscal themes. Six chapters in Luke (16-21) are notable for their numerous references to money. We have time and space here to touch on one or two things from each chapter.

Chapter 16 contains a parable whose point is not readily grasped. Read it through in verses 1-8. The purpose of the tale seems to be not the business methods of the manager (steward) for these were dubious, but the wisdom of using money with an eye on eternity. Verse 9 is the key. Jesus appears to be saying that the right use of money in this life—giving it away to the needy or spending it selflessly—will win you friends whom you may meet only in heaven, presumably those whose plight your money has helped to ease. Verse 10 is important too. Jesus contrasts honesty with dishonesty in both large and small matters. To deal dishonestly with a trivial sum betrays a lack of suitability for the conferring of a greater trust.

Chapter 17 holds little by way of explicit reference to

money but verses 3b and 4 present our Lord's command concerning the duty to forgive repeatedly. The number seven in Jewish thought represents perfection or completeness and so forgiving seven times means perpetual forgiveness. This is perhaps clearer in Matthew's version of the command which you can find in Matthew 18:21, 22 (GNB, KJV) where the "seven" becomes "seventy times seven." A dramatic parable then follows, highlighting the risks of failure to deal with others on the basis of a generous and forgiving spirit. Applying this specifically to money matters, it is obvious that as Christians we cannot insist on our strict legal rights, especially in one-to-one dealings with fellow Christians or with those worse off than ourselves. Because Christians are forgiven people, they are called to be forgiving. It is not hard to imagine a circumstance in which carrying this out will mean losing money to which we are, strictly speaking, otherwise entitled. Jesus gave up more than this for us.

In chapter 18, we encounter the rich young ruler with his question in verse 18, a question which echoes through the centuries and which is still the heart cry of fallen humanity: "What must I do to inherit eternal life?" Jesus warmed to this questioner and saw much potential in him (Mark 10:21). He was interested in spiritual things. Jesus invited him to follow, making the condition plain: "Sell everything you have and give to the poor, and you will have treasure in heaven." Note two things: a) this is not a command to all Christians in the world to impoverish themselves, but a specific remedy for this individual whose money stood between him and a living trust in God; b) the tragic loss to the kingdom of all the potential Jesus saw in this young man, so much so that we wonder just what he could have achieved for God if only he could have learned to hold loosely his worldly assets.

Chapter 19 brings to us the marvelously contrasting figure of Zacchaeus (verses 1-9). What the rich young ruler could not bring himself to do, Zacchaeus volunteered to do, clambering down in haste from his sycamore tree to usher Jesus into his home. When Jesus found Zacchaeus, Zacchaeus found himself! How do we know? Suddenly, money was no longer the biggest thing in his life!

In Chapter 20 we find Jesus ready to acknowledge sensible obligations about paying taxes to public funds (verses 19-26). Verse 25 is well known: "Give to Caesar what is Caesar's, and to God what is God's." Although Jesus knew and warned about the folly of idolizing money and making the pursuit of it life's central purpose, he was pragmatic too. After all, the disciples kept funds for every day necessities (John 13:29). It is true that when he sent them out in pairs to go ahead of him (see Luke 10:1-12) he told them to take no money, but this must be seen against the culture of that time which included a duty of hospitality to itinerant religious teachers, and Jesus' instructions to the disciples make reference to this. His words in Luke 20:25 leave no doubt that he recognized fiscal obligations to the state. In the same breath, he reminded his questioners of their obligations to God, which would have included monetary obligations but which money alone could not satisfy.

Chapter 21 opens with one of the most moving, challenging episodes in the New Testament. At the entrance to the temple courtyard in Jerusalem there were placed large vase-shaped receptacles into which those using the temple placed their dues. Voluntary gifts could also be given. The rich came with their large gifts and remained rich. The impoverished widow came with her two tiny coins, rendering herself penniless. In God's eyes, her coins were more valuable than the superficially impressive donations of the wealthy. This brings us now face to face with the burning issue of just how much we should give to God's work.

How much?

There is only one broad answer to the question of how much we should give to God's work. We should give as much as we possibly can, everything we can afford, and even what we cannot afford. After all, nothing we have is truly our own. It is all God's anyway.

Many Christians practice tithing. This is the regular setting aside of a tenth of your income so that it can be given to God, usually through a regular gift to your place of worship. Some divide the tithe, giving a portion to their place of worship and the rest to other Christian causes such as missionary work. Many who tithe give additional free-will offerings, or love-offerings, on special occasions or in response to special appeals or needs.

You need to be aware that there is no general agreement among Christians about tithing. Some find it a hard and onerous thing to do, feeling they cannot afford a tenth of what they have. Some feel a tenth is far too little and they regularly give a lot more, a third or a half of their income.

Let me be very clear. I have no hesitation at all in recommending to you, a new Christian, the practice of tithing. It will get you off to a good start, inculcating good habits, and will allow you to obey the New Testament principle of giving to God's work with regularity, week by week or month by month (see 1 Corinthians 16:2).

Nevertheless, it is important that you are fully informed on the matter and so below I set out the main considerations, both for and against. Let's note the negative considerations first:

1. All the Scriptural commands on tithing are found in the Old Testament, e.g. Malachi 3:10, 11.

2. The Old Testament verses dealing with personal giving are so numerous and so diverse that it would take considerable scholarship and a very detailed comparison of all the passages to clarify whatever might be binding on modern Christians.

3. Nowhere in the New Testament are Christians told, or even encouraged, to tithe.

4. In fact, the few New Testament references to tithing crop up in negative contexts. A self-righteous Pharisee seems to think his habit of tithing makes him right with God (Luke 18:11, 12), and Jesus criticizes other Pharisees who tithe meticulously but ignore more fundamental social and spiritual duties (Luke 11:42).

These four points are arguments against tithing that are commonly raised and, on the face of them they are fairly plausible. I have just a faint suspicion, however, that when I have heard them they have been used as pretexts for giving *less* than a tenth to God. Had they come from those who were regularly giving more than a tenth I would have been more impressed! So let's look at the positive side now, taking the four points in the same order:

1. The Old Testament is still the inspired and authoritative word of God to us, even though we have the New Testament too. We cannot dismiss the Old Testament as though it is somehow less valid now that Jesus has come.

2. It is true that Jewish religious laws on giving were, and still are, complex. However, this much is clear—at the root of the system lay the principle of the tithe. It was simple to calculate and provided a pragmatic point of reference for giving back to God a portion of what he had graciously bestowed. It also made possible and practical, no doubt, the forecasting of future temple and other revenues so that forward-planning could be undertaken for building and other projects.

3. Silence in the New Testament upon a matter to which the earlier documents of the Old Testament give some prominence cannot be assumed to indicate rejection or dissent. It could very well be a sign of continuing to accept what was seen to be a basic and obvious requirement, so obvious that it needed neither instructions nor arguments in its favor. Neither can we assume that the first Christians abandoned their legal obligations to give as good Jews, according to the laws of Moses. This might explain the New Testament's apparent emphasis upon freewill offerings (e.g. 2 Corinthians

8:2-5), giving over and above the basic tenth, the tenth going to the temple revenues and the freewill offerings being used for the needs of the specifically Christian community. Our information on patterns of personal giving among the first century Christians is at best scanty, and so what is said here is pretty speculative. However, I repeat that the absence of unambiguous commands to Christians to tithe cannot automatically be taken as a New Testament rejection of the tithing norm. To command it may have been seen as a statement, at that time, of the blindingly obvious!

4. The references by Jesus to tithing contain no hint at all of criticism of tithing itself. What Jesus condemns is the elevation of outward religious gestures at the expense of true and inner religion of the heart. Giving to God is pleasing in his sight only if it comes from a life that is in a right relationship to him.

It will be seen, therefore, that the usual arguments against tithing are not as convincing as might first seem to be the case. Apart from the well-established place the tithe holds in Scripture, there is massive empirical evidence (evidence drawn from practical experience) that where the people tithe, God pours out his blessings upon them. A few years ago the Moody Bible Institute in Chicago compiled letters written by Christians who had begun to tithe. Published in book form and entitled *I Tithe Joyfully!* these letters pulsate with thanksgiving to God for his abundant blessings. They are the living testimonies of Christians from every kind of background. They give a tenth of their income to God and some give much more. The giving comes from wages, investments, state benefits, pensions, student grants and even from the pocket-money of a child.

In the matter of personal giving, start as you mean to go on. You cannot afford not to give regularly and systematically. I encourage you wholeheartedly to adopt the habit of tithing. The Lord honors those who honor him.

Being God's trustee

When you are a Christian you come to see material possessions in a new light. Yes, you still own things, whether few or many, small or large. But your ownership is according to this world's laws. Your eyes now are on a more distant horizon and you realize that "the earth is the Lord's, and everything in it" (Psalm 24:1). So if you have money, it is all God's money. If you have land, it is God's land. If you have books, or a car, or clothing, they are all God's things. You have possession of them, but they are ultimately God's. He has granted them to you as his trustee or steward. You are looking after them for him, using them according to his will.

This is an insight which, while very definitely for Christians, emerged much earlier than the Christian era. Read, for instance, 1 Chronicles 29 and the account of David and Solomon gathering materials to build the temple of God. Verses 6-9 list what was given: gold, silver, bronze, iron, precious stones, all in great amounts. However, it is the dedicatory prayer of King David in verses 10-19 which captures the attention: "Lord God ... everything in heaven and earth is yours ... Wealth and honor come from you .... Who am I, and who are my people, that we should be able to give as generously as this? Everything comes from you and we have given only what comes from your hand."

So everything we have, not just a tenth, is his. We do not say, "A tenth is God's, the rest is mine!" We say, "It all belongs to God, but a tenth or more will be used specifically to build his spiritual kingdom here on earth."

A good steward, a good trustee, sees the needs of others and responds with whatever assets are at hand. The money does not get hoarded, the cupboards do not bulge with unused goods, and the house is not always a shining model of tidiness because no children or visitors come in. Everything is at God's disposal. There is no more practical test of our holiness and of our love and devotion to the Lord than how we use the money and possessions he has given us. One Christian thinker, Frederick Mitchell, put it like this: "The world asks how much we own; Christ asks how we use it. The world thinks more of getting; Christ thinks more of giving. The world asks what we give; Christ asks how we give. Men ask how much we give; the Bible how much we keep. To the unconverted, money is a means of gratification; to the converted, a means of grace; to the one an opportunity of comfort, to the other an opportunity of consecration."

Take my silver and my gold,
Not a mite would I withhold

CHAPTER 10

Being yourself while building bridges

Can I Witness?

An important distinction

There are two words often used in Christian circles as though they mean the same. One is "witnessing," the other is "evangelizing." Much misunderstanding can be avoided if you grasp from the outset that being a *witness to* Christ is not the same as being an *evangelist for* Christ.

Every Christian is a witness. Like it or not, we cannot avoid it. Once it is known that we have turned to Christ and are following his example and teaching, everything we do witnesses (bears testimony) to the sincerity or otherwise of our Christianity. Moreover, there will be occasions when we simply long to speak up, with words of witness, in a specific way about our faith and our personal experience of discipleship. In extreme cases, we may even be compelled to witness (Luke 21:12-19).

This is not the same as being an evangelist. There is a separate gift of the Spirit known as the gift of evangelism and it is not given to everyone (see Ephesians 4:11; 2 Timothy 4:5; Acts 21:8). There was a distinct order of evangelists in the early church whose task was to preach the gospel and lead others into a clearcut commitment to Jesus Christ as Lord. This spiritual gift is still given to some believers today. The Holy Spirit empowers them to speak and act (often on a one-to-one basis) with special boldness and courage in leading unbelievers to the point where a definite conversion experience takes place.

While witnessing and evangelizing can be distinguished in this way, it is obvious that they are linked and may sometimes overlap. For instance, a Christian gifted by God for evangelism bears the same duty as every believer to be a good witness, both in word and deed. (In theory, it is possible for someone with the gift of evangelism to be a bad witness because of behavior faults or a lack of Christlike love.) Much evangelism is done only on a foundation already laid by the faithful witnessing of Christians who may not have the specific gift of evangelism. It is as though one sows and another reaps (John 4:34-38).

A grasp of this basic distinction is helpful. Masses of Christians carry feelings of guilt because they have never actually led another person into faith in Christ. It is important to relieve those guilt feelings and liberate such believers by a reminder that not everyone is gifted by God in an identical way (see chapters 6 and 7 above). The calling of every Christian to bear witness to Christ ought not to be confused with the gifting of some Christians of evangelism (see again John 4:34-38).

Scripture

It is helpful, in appreciating our responsibilities as witnesses, to look at the Scriptures. Second Corinthians 4:13, 14 shows why we witness to Christ: "It is written: 'I believed; therefore I have spoken.' With that same spirit of faith we also believe and therefore speak, because we know the one who raised the Lord Jesus from the dead will also raise us with Jesus." We witness, therefore, because we believe and we know the truth about Jesus. There is an exceptionally beautiful statement earlier in the same letter of Paul at 2:14, 15 which offers a wonderful image of what witnessing is about. We are told that God uses us to make the knowledge about Christ spread everywhere like a sweet "fragrance." "For we are to God the aroma of Christ among those who are being saved and those who are perishing." Marvelous!

The notion of vast numbers of human witnesses to the Lord on earth goes back to the Old Testament. We find God speaking through the prophet Isaiah to the entire nation of Israel, saying: "You are my witnesses ... and my servant whom I have chosen" (Isaiah 43:10). With the birth of the Christian Church, this duty transferred to all who trust in Jesus. He promised unambiguously that the Holy Spirit would come upon his followers and fill them with power for the precise purpose of witnessing to him (Acts 1:8). This was gloriously fulfilled on the Day of Pentecost (Acts 2). The same Holy Spirit motivates Christians today for witnessing to the same Lord Jesus Christ. Read and take personal encouragement from the words of Jesus recorded in John 15:26, 27.

Be yourself

Quite probably your very first attempts to witness by word of mouth will prove costly to you. There will be some fear perhaps—fear of being laughed at or of simply being rejected. Do not be afraid. God is with you and alive in you. This is the God who told a hesitant and nervous Moses: "Is it not I, the Lord. Now, go! I will help you speak, and will teach you what to say" (Exodus 4:11, 12). What he did for Moses, he can do for you.

You may experience shyness. No problem! Just witness shyly! You may falter in your speech. So witness falteringly! The Lord can use your hesitant words which spring from a sincere heart more easily than brash, self-confident words which rely more on the speaker's human talents than the Lord's assistance.

So do not allow yourself to be put off by initial awkwardness. The best thing is just being yourself. Naturalness is very attractive. Talking naturally about your religious experience without lapsing into jargon and without sounding sanctimonious or pious is attractive too.

You can talk to family and friends about your faith or about religious matters generally in the same way you would chat about everyday things such as work, vacations, children, studies, etc. Above all, be yourself. Do not envy another's gifts. You are you, and God likes you. If you witness obediently, even in weakness, he will honor you for it.

No one is beyond reach

No witness is ever wasted, because no one is beyond the reach of the gospel. There is a capacity in every person to respond to the good news about Christ. Someone once said that within every person there is a space waiting to be filled and that space is God-shaped. Deep in every human heart, sometimes so deep that it seems things are hopeless, there is a longing to be good. Even in lives that look as though they are beyond repair, there is a spark that can be rekindled, a hunger for God and for goodness that can be reawakened. Your life, your witness can be used by the Holy Spirit as another link in the chain that will lead at last to a coming home to God for someone.

Let's change the metaphor from being links in a chain to being bridges. Witnessing can be thought of as building bridges between the Lord and an unsaved person. Research shows that over 90% of new Christians come to faith as the result of a friendship with a Christian. The friendship is the bridge over which an unsaved person can walk into forgiveness and a knowledge of Jesus as Savior.

A few years ago I listened to a young Jewish girl telling her story. At that time she had been a Christian for 18 months. A Jew by birth, she had married in the synagogue. Then a series of sorrows struck. She lost her child. Her husband left her. Her parents reacted to her with coldness. Scarcely knowing where to turn, she went to stay with a friend at Southend in the English county of Essex. Her friend was a Salvationist and invited her to come to the worship service on Sunday. There she found her Savior, kneeling as a seeker at the mercy seat. She spoke of the peace that came to her and, although her understanding was then limited, also of her desires to discover and follow God's will for her life. As she spoke, she was radiant.

Now two things stand out from this account. The first is the witness of her Salvationist friend resulting in the crucial invitation to come with her to her place of worship. We are reminded of the Samaritan woman who met Jesus and returned to her friends saying simply, "Come, see" (John 4:29). Many did and many believed (John 4:41). The second is that people can be highly receptive to the gospel when they are in trouble. Sometimes we see ourselves and our need truly for the first time when all human and material support has been stripped away. It can occur in illness, or in marital distress, in unemployment, or in the death of a loved one. The Lord is courteous, of course, and never pushes in uninvited. Neither should his followers seek callously to take advantage of someone's sorrow. But if a person turns to a Christian friend for comfort in distress, natural opportunities will open up for gently discussing spiritual things. Those opportunities should always be taken.

Taking opportunities, like Andrew

It is open to you to pray about having general opportunities to witness, asking for eyes to see them when they come along. Pray too for wisdom and courage and the right words to suit each occasion.

We have a good role model in Andrew, the disciple of Jesus. There are three instances recorded in John's Gospel where he displays a keen sense of opportunism about introducing people to Jesus. In John 1:35-42 we see him captivated by the thought of Jesus being the

Lamb of God. After spending most of a day in the Lord's company, he went at once to find his brother, Simon Peter. "We have found the Messiah," he told him (verse 41). Five short words to whet his brother's appetite. "And he brought him to Jesus" (verse 42). Six short words to denote the most loving thing one person can do for another. When Jesus set eyes on Simon, he knew at once that here was the man who, despite setbacks to come, would be a rock for the things of God and the upbuilding of the early Church after Pentecost.

How precious to Andrew must have been the knowledge, as he watched his brother's life and relationship with Jesus unfold through the years, that it was his initiative which put Simon into the presence of Jesus in the first place. We can never know all that may flow from our faithfulness in witnessing. Andrew's action is an inspiration also to all who long to see their loved ones come to Christ. If your witness to your family members seems unfruitful, never forget the power of prayer. I knew a lady in Bulawayo, Zimbabwe, who prayed for 16 years for her husband to respond to Christ. Her prayers were answered. Imagine her joy, having worshipped Sunday after Sunday without him at her side for 16 years!

We next notice Andrew when Jesus was followed by a big crowd, curious to see some miracle or other (John 6:1-13). Out all day, the crowd wanted food. It was Andrew who spotted a young boy with bread and fish. Five thousand were miraculously fed. The nameless boy has gone down in Christian history as the carrier of the world's most talked-about sack lunch! It was Andrew who spotted him, but it was the Lord who saw all the potential in what the boy had. Just so, our part is to focus attention on Jesus. The Holy Spirit in us brings this about (John 15:26), helping us to speak about our Lord. If we are faithful witnesses, wonderful consequences can follow. Human souls, hungering for God, can be satisfied.

The third episode is found in John 12:20-26 when some Greek inquirers approached Philip, wanting to meet Jesus. It was Andrew to whom Philip turned for guidance. Together they took the request to Jesus (verse 22) and reported the interest shown by the Greeks. Jesus is Lord of all races and all peoples. Andrew knew it. After all, he had been given a Greek name, even though he was born a Jew. The Holy Spirit was pleased to honor his ability to be an introducer of people to Jesus, a builder of bridges—for a family member, a youngster and even for strangers from another land.

Witnessing without words

I do not want to convey the impression that all forms of witnessing involve speaking. Many do, but not all. Yes, the Scriptures say clearly: "Always be prepared to give an answer to everyone who asks you to give the reason for the hope that you have" (1 Peter 3:15). We are, moreover, to do this "with gentleness and respect" (3:15). No aggressive, intimidating and embarrassing buttonholing of people as they go about their everyday lives!

However, there are ways of being a witness to Christ that are non-verbal. Discover them and use them if the Lord so prompts you. A few examples may help.

Some Christians use a sticker on their car. Some wear a lapel badge or pin. I know a Christian university teacher, Derek, who covenanted with the Lord to wear a "fish" pin. This is a modern replica of the old secret sign used by persecuted Christians in the first century A.D. The Greek for "fish" was *ichthus*, these letters representing *Iesus* (Jesus), *Christos* (Christ), *theou* (of God), *(h)uios* (son), *soter* (Savior). Derek asked God to give him a clear opening at least once a week to explain the meaning of his pin. God answered his prayer. Here then is an example of a non-verbal witness leading to an opportunity for spoken witness.

The uniform worn by many Salvationists is another example of witnessing by action rather than words. All who see it (or almost all) know that its wearer represents the things of God. Wearing it brings a tremendous responsibility to live out in practice all that it stands for, and to justify the remarkable trust shown by members of the public in the Army uniform.

The most telling witness of all is your life lived in holiness and purity by the grace and power of God. Christians are observed closely by others. They will be quick to notice even a hint of hypocrisy or double standards. My paternal grandfather, an Englishman, worked as a supervisor in the docks in Goole, Yorkshire. All his men knew he was a Salvationist and they would see him in his uniform marching the streets of Goole with the Army band and speaking in the open-air meetings. Sometimes he would reflect aloud about this. "They watch me more closely than they watch the local priest," he would say. He knew the power and value of a consistent Christian life. Imagine the damage to the Kingdom's reputation if he had ever been known to let his Lord down!

Witnessing, then, is not always about words. Your actions speak louder than words. Never let those around you say, "I cannot hear you, because your actions drown out your words!"

Can you witness? Yes, you can! Will they listen? Yes, they will! Will they jeer, will they sneer? Some will! Does it matter? Not a bit! Be yourself. Be a builder of bridges to Christ.

CHAPTER 11

How God Guides

What About My Job, My Studies?

Some commonsense principles

Becoming a Christian is the most significant thing you will ever do in your life. It affects everything. Your whole outlook changes. However, that does not mean that you need to rush into big decisions about your job or your studies. God will guide you in these things.

First and foremost, note what Paul said to the new Christians in the city of Corinth: "Each one should retain the place in life the Lord assigned to him and to which God has called him. This is the rule I lay down in all the churches ... Each one should remain in the situation which he was in when God called him" (1 Corinthians 7:17-24). Aquila and Priscilla did not stop manufacturing tents when they were saved (Acts 18:1-3). Onesimus went on being a slave, only now a Christian slave

(Colossians 4:9; Philemon). Cornelius continued as a Roman centurion (Acts 10), and Sergius Paulus went on working as the governor of Cyprus (Acts 13:6-12). Lydia's cloth-manufacturing business (Acts 16:14, 40) went on running. Even the jailer at Philippi appears to have stayed in his post (Acts 16), but no doubt his prison was a different place! It is vitally important that God has his people serving him faithfully in secular settings.

Having stressed this, we ought to recognize exceptions to the rule. There are two broad categories of situations in which a Christian would have to give up his or her present position. The first is where a vocation to full-time Christian service is received. The second is where a Christian works in a job which is directly incompatible with the things of Christ.

If Lydia and the jailer (Acts 16) continued in their professions, it would have been impossible for the third convert at Philippi to do so. This was the slave girl who told fortunes for her money-hungry bosses. Some ways of earning a living are at odds with being a Christian and so some jobs must be left behind by a new Christian. Anything connected with sexual immorality is an obvious example. The gambling industry, alcohol sales or promotions and the tobacco industry come readily to mind. So do occupations which in any way exploit human weaknesses.

Choice of career is often determined when we are young. It may be influenced by family connections, by the schools we attend, or simply by the first main job opportunity to crop up when our full time education ceases. Most people are motivated in their choice also by salary structures, promotion and status prospects, job security or by whatever degree of personal aptitude they have for the work involved. Becoming a Christian involves reassessing these motives. A Christian belongs to God. While being aware of obligations to earn a living and to provide for dependents, we cannot choose selfishly or as the world would choose. The basic question for a Christian selecting a career is not "How much can I earn?" or "How high will I rise?" but rather "How can I maximize my usefulness to God?" William Booth said, "Your days at the most cannot be very long, so use them to the best of your ability for the glory of God and the benefit of your generation."

It is time to think about the ways in which God guides believers in making right choices and in the overall shape and direction of their lives.

Divine guidance

Become the kind of Christian who is aware of and open to God's guidance. Seek this daily. God's people have always done so. The writer of Psalm 25 cries out: "Show me your ways, O Lord, teach me your paths; guide me in your truth" (verses 4, 5). The Lord has always responded by giving guidance to the faithful and the meek. Again, this is the psalmist's experience: "He leads me beside quiet waters, he restores my soul. He guides me in paths of righteousness for his name's sake" (Psalm 23:2, 3).

How does guidance come? Here are some things to take into account:

1. The most frequent means God uses is our reading of *Scripture*. Most of our guidance is obtained in this

way, especially as the character and spirit of Jesus are revealed to us and as we seek to follow in his steps.

2. Guidance can come also through the *expository preaching* of the Scriptures. Sometimes you will feel that the preacher is speaking only to you and for you. Be very open to the Holy Spirit if this occurs.

3. God also uses the wise and mature *counsel* of other experienced Christians. Often this will come from your spiritual leaders, at other times from a godly friend. Be willing to ask more experienced Christians, especially your leaders, for guidance. God can use such conversations to clarify your thoughts with his light.

4. God guides his people also by means of *circumstances*. Sometimes doors of opportunity open and close to us. We need to sense the hand of God in this at times. Guidance through circumstances will be perceived clearly only if we are alive to God in our prayer life and if we are paying attention to the Scriptures.

5. Sometimes we get a *deep inner conviction* about a course of action being either right or wrong. Waiting on God in prayer may cause the conviction to increase until it is an abiding and steady inner sureness of heart. Guidance about a vocation to full-time service often comes in this way (see further below).

6. Remember that God has given you reasoning powers. Use them. If you are placing every bit of yourself at his disposal, you will eventually be able to trust the Holy Spirit to guide you through *sanctified common sense*. The great John Wesley (see chapter 4) said that God usually guided him by presenting sensible reasons to his mind for some proposed course of action.

7. Very occasionally, God guides in *some exceptional way*, such as in a dream or vision. New Christians ought not to seek for such things. They are rare and seem to be used by God only in extreme circumstances when much is at stake for the sake of the gospel. God can, of course, use any means to keep our feet on the path of his choosing, but more often than not he will nudge us along steadily but surely, using unspectacular methods.

8. From all that has been said above, the reasons for any *feeling of a lack of guidance* should be obvious: inattention to Scripture; neglect of taking things to God in prayer; a refusal to accept humbly and patiently the circumstances of everyday life; a lack of meekness or willingness to learn; fear of change or of the future or perhaps a basic lack of trust in God.

Nearly 400 years ago Paulus Gerhardt, a godly man, wrote these verses about trusting God for guidance:

> *Who points the clouds their course,*
> *Whom winds and seas obey,*
> *He shall direct thy wandering feet,*
> *He shall prepare thy way.*
>
> *No profit canst thou gain*
> *By self-consuming care;*
> *To him commend thy cause, his ear*
> *Attends the softest prayer.*
>
> *Thy everlasting truth*
> *Father, thy ceaseless love*
> *Sees all thy children's wants, and knows*
> *What best for each will prove.*

A calling to full-time service

How does such a calling come? To whom does it come? When does it come? What do I do if it comes? These and a host of other questions deserve answering. We have space to touch only upon the more important issues, so please do not regard what follows as a comprehensive treatise on the subject of religious vocations! Nevertheless, a few helpful things can be said with new Christians in mind.

First, you already are in fact a full-time Christian. You are both full time and, I hope, wholehearted. This does not mean that you are to resign from your job, or give up your studies, to rush into the ministry.

Let me offer a word here to any student readers. If you have come to Christ as a student, you are in a setting which might place considerable pressures and temptations upon you, but you have at your feet also priceless opportunities for sensible and natural witnessing. What has been said earlier about Christians staying in their present jobs unless there are compelling reasons not to, applies equally to new Christians engaged upon a course of study. See your studies through. Be a fine Christian student. Use your mind for God, thanking him for your gifts of intellect. Work diligently. Let your experience of Christ show itself in your powers of concentration, your attention to detail in study assignments and in the general orderliness of your life. Offer your studies to the Lord as a gift placed before him. Ask him to use your qualifications for his purposes in your life and for the benefit of others.

If your studies are nearly complete, consider your

career options as a Christian should. If some inner conviction has taken root about full-time Christian work or ministry, make an early approach to your Christian leaders to discuss it, but recognize the need for experience in some secular work first. Those who screen candidates for full time work will look for experience of the wider world and a proven track record of integrity in that setting. So too will those to whom one day you may minister and whom you may lead.

Any Christian person's sense of being called by God to leave a secular career for full-time ministry needs to be subjected to testing. Your own convictions may run deep. That is an essential precondition. Nevertheless, your calling must be sensitively, but also rigorously, tested and all Christian denominations have ways of going about this. Submit yourself humbly to the process. Remember that offering yourself is not enough. Your suitability and your personal convictions need to be recognized by the body of Christ, the body of believers generally. Your local church or corps leaders will thus be asked about you. They will share their views as to your general standing as a believer, the quality of your Christian service in your local setting, your character, your gifts and your potential for Christ in full time service. Interviews will follow. Then more interviews! More reports and references from other Christians and spiritual leaders who know you. In this way, you are chosen by the body, not merely set loose for ministry as a result of your own subjective feelings.

What sort of women and men are looked for? Well, obviously, it helps to be fit and healthy. But more important are qualities of heart, mind and spirit. People of character and of integrity are needed. Cleverness is not enough. A good education may help but of itself is insufficient. Lack of it should be no automatic bar, but minimum standards will be set down. Meekness and teachableness are vital qualities. So too is respect for others (and not only for one's superiors!). Above all, if you are to be a soul-winner, there must be a longing to see people saved. I do not mean by this just a general interest in the Church growing larger or The Salvation Army increasing its membership. These are legitimate and commendable goals but by themselves will not serve as adequate springs for a lifetime of service in full time ministry. We are speaking here of a heart so on fire with a love for unsaved people that to win them for the Lord you will be willing to forfeit much, and then much more again—leisure, rest, reputation, family connections, earning power or status (even in the Army or in your church).

It is a willingness to spend oneself and be spent for the sake of the gospel. Are you ready for a life of sacrifice? Not sacrifice for the sake of it, but for the sake of others and the Lord Jesus Christ. This way, sacrifice is reward. It is all gain.

To enter upon such a path you have to be very sure. "Don't do it, son," my godly parents said to me when first I told them that I felt convinced of my calling. "Don't do it, not if there is some other way you can be happy." Wise counsel. There was no other way for me. I just knew that if I did not offer myself for consideration, I would regret it for ever. I have not the faintest regret today. Scars, yes! Regrets, none! It is my testimony that finally saying "yes" to God, when working as a young academic lawyer, goes today to the very root of my walk with the Lord. Obedience is the key to spiritual progress. Samuel Logan Brengle writes of "the silken bridle" of God's will. To wear it is a priceless thing.

Some respond reluctantly to God's call. Moses was like this. Others say "yes" at once, as did Isaiah. To all alike God says: "I am with you always" (Matthew 28:20); "My Presence will go with you, and I will give you rest" (Exodus 33:14); "I am with you, and will rescue you" (Jeremiah 1:19).

God's will for you can never harm you. If you sense the "oughtness" of God's voice, saying that he knows you would like to be this or that, but that you "ought" to preach, to serve, to lead, to minister, to spend and be spent, remember that God's plan has been, and forever will be, absolutely right for you. Never let your thinking compromise on the integrity and perfection of God or of his gracious ways with human beings. Recognize just as clearly too that you must serve if you want to reign. You must yield if you want victory. You must be tied if you want freedom. Dash to pieces the fake god of independence. A kite might think it could kiss the very stars if only that hand would let it go! But cut the string, and see the kite crash to the ground! The hand that guides us is the hand that sustains us. Cut loose and you are finished.

God is calling men and women all over the world to serve him in full time ministry. In Korea, Chun Chaikook received his call as a third-year high school student and after attending revival meetings. He started to preach in open air meetings and found that people responded. In Italy, Angela Dentico attended summer Bible camps and there God stirred her heart. Derek Dolling came across a beach meeting in Weymouth, England, and knew at once a sense of God's call. Ken Hawken was in the UK's Royal Air Force when a call which he describes as "vivid and real" came to him. Israel Lengoasa was at a commissioning and ordination ceremony for Salvation Army officers in South Africa and God used that occasion to show him the pattern his own life should take. Still others testify to a sense of calling which they trace back to childhood years, a calling often confirmed by God in later maturity. All these were called by God to "guard the truth" (2 Timothy 1:14, RSV) and to pass it on obediently to saved and unsaved alike in their preaching and teaching for Christ.

What about you?

Not every Christian is called to full-time ministry. Every Christian is, however, required to be open to God's voice, and especially those who appear eligible by age and aptitude for wider service. Is God calling you? Or are you drifting along comfortably? Remember what Booth said: "Your days at most cannot be very long, so use them."

Henry Martyn was a student who achieved brilliant success in college. He was ordained as a Church of England priest to an impoverished parish. He could have had an outstanding academic career. At 24 he set out for India. It took him a year to get there. He died at

31 years of age. In the meantime he translated the New Testament into Hindustani, Arabic and Persian! When he left England, he had only one quarter of his life left. He used it. Use yours too. It may be long or short. Just make it count!

CHAPTER 12

Stepping out in faith

Can I Really Rely on God?

Eternal and unbroken promises

God has never let anyone down. He is not going to fail you. This is the core truth that holds the very universe in place—the absolute, one hundred percent certainty that God is faithful. He has not beckoned you to take up your cross and follow him only suddenly to turn and change his mind! He does not toy with us. What he begins, he completes.

"The Lord is faithful" is the proclamation of the Scriptures (2 Thessalonians 3:3). And again: "He remains faithful, because he cannot be false to himself" (2 Timothy 2:13).

His promises are therefore like no others. They are from everlasting to everlasting. In all of time, and of eternity too, not one has been broken. A new Christian has the world at his feet. Better still, his feet stand safe and sure upon the promises of God. Hear again the Lord's solemn undertaking to go with you and never to leave you:

1. *I will be with you* (Exodus 3:12).

2. *I will be with you; I will never leave you nor forsake you ... the Lord Your God will be with you wherever you go* (Joshua 1:5, 9).

3. *I am with you always, to the very end of the age* (Matthew 28:20).

4. *God has said, "Never will I leave you; never will I forsake you." So we say with confidence, "The Lord is my helper, I will not be afraid. What can man do to me?"* (Hebrews 13:5, 6).

These promises are for all who love and trust him. The praising poetry of the psalms comes back time and time again to the faithfulness of God. Friends may fail us. Business colleagues too. Even family may let us down. But never God! "The Lord is faithful to all his promises," sings David in Psalm 145:13. "He remains faithful forever" is the echo of Psalm 146:6.

This knowledge is the foundation of a life of faith and trust: first, knowing God is unswervingly reliable in a way no human could ever be; then, stepping out in faith knowing he is ahead of us, beside and behind us, above and below us, and even indwelling us too. Never let go of this.

Cosmic companionship

All the great men and women of God have had an abiding sense of God's presence in their lives. When they needed him most, he was there. Some of these people have been mentioned earlier in chapter 4. Among them was Dr. Martin Luther King, Jr. Seven years before he was murdered in Memphis, Tennessee, he visited England to be interviewed on television. He talked about his childhood, his love for his father and mother and his early awareness of color differences. He spoke also of his adult career and his calling into ministry. Then he described how it felt to receive death threats to both himself and his loved ones. He spoke openly about fear and loneliness. What had helped him through? A feeling of not being abandoned, he said. The phrase he used is unforgettable: he said he felt "a sense of cosmic companionship." Don't you sense this too? I do, and am glad, for it is God keeping his promise.

Playing your part

A lot has been said in earlier chapters to indicate just what is expected of you—by the Lord and by your fellow believers too! There are three verses in 1 Peter chapter 1 which seem to sum it all up in a trilogy of pungent exhortations:

Verse 13: Prepare your mind for action. The verse goes on at once with a warning about staying alert. It is a call for mental readiness to do spiritual battle. Taken literally, the verse says, "Gird up the loins of your mind!" Imagine a man in a heavy robe down to his ankles. He wants to run, so what must he do? He must bundle up the skirts of the robe between his legs and tuck it into his belt! Then he runs! So, the exhortation is to be ready to move into action. Be alert and watchful. Be on your guard. Look at 4:7 and 5:8, which speak of (a) alertness in prayer and (b) alertness in temptation.

Verse 14: Be an obedient child of God. The command to us here is to be children of obedience. In chapter 11 it was emphasized that obedience to God is the key to spiritual progress. You cannot obey unless first you wait for God and listen. Only then can you hear him. Thus will he lead you further away from your old desires and closer to new and changed ambitions.

Verse 15: Be holy in all you do. Why? Because God is holy (verse 16). So once again the call to a holy life reaches our ears. You are holy by status because you are saved and are Christ's. But being holy in name only is not enough. His Holy Spirit, cultivating spiritual fruits within you, is going to work out your newfound status in practical results. Your personality and your actions will change more and more to reflect those of your Lord.

So, play your part and God will perform his. Be alert, be obedient, be holy.

God's university

Stepping out in faith requires also that you remain teachable, going on and on learning about God and his ways. You are enrolled, as it were, in God's university. I recall an old Christian gentleman once claiming that he had his B.A. "I'm Born Again" was his disarming argument! He went on to claim his M.A. too! Marvelously

Altered! Well, you have your spiritual B.A. already. How about going for the M.A.? You can get it in God's university. Psalm 25 could be the prospectus. Open your Bible to it now and check for the following details:

1. *Making application.* You must earnestly and sincerely plead, "Show me, teach me ..." (verses 4, 5).

2. *Chief faculty member.* The person in charge is the Lord, the God who saves and who can be trusted (verses 4, 5).

3. *Teaching method.* Anything the Lord needs to do to instruct sinners (verse 8).

4. *Staff qualifications.* a) Being divinely righteous and good (verse 8) b) being kind and showing a constant love (verse 6).

5. *Who can enroll?* Sinners (verse 8); the humble (verse 9); those who have a reverence for the Lord (verse 12).

6. *Courses available.* a) The path sinners should follow (verse 8); b) God's will (verse 9); c) living according to the truth (verse 5); d) the ways of God (verse 4).

7. *Free extras offered.* a) Being led by God (verse 9); b) being befriended by God (verse 14). These courses are conditional upon the student being humble (verse 9) and obedient (verse 10).

8. *Career prospects for graduates.* Being safe (v. 20)!

There is no finer learning institution than this. It is open to everyone. Take full advantage of it. You can attend it all your life, sitting at the Master's feet. Yet you can never learn it all. Somehow, the more you learn from him, the more you realize how little you know. The more time you spend at his feet, the more you realize how unlike him you are. Often your gaze will be fixed upon those strange, dark marks in his feet, until your eyes move up to follow the movements of his gloriously disfigured hands. Then your heart will feel almost at breaking point as waves of sorrow, love and gratitude sweep through you. "The marks were made for me. For me!" That thought will close all others out and your single impulse will be to kneel in homage to adore him. In this university the students are allowed to kneel, for at its heart is a Mercy Seat, a holy trysting place, where words of eternal love are whispered deep within our souls. In this university, if you would learn, then you must kneel.

Venite adoremus!
Come let us adore him!

Last words

I want to end this book with three things which I offer to you, the reader, in Christian love: a word of testimony, a word of encouragement and a word of prayer.

First, the testimony. I offer to you words written in a letter to me by a young Christian leader. I hope they echo in your soul. "Just let me have my Jesus, and I have what nothing else in the world can give—acceptance without achieving, satisfaction with stillness, somewhere I can experience grace in failure, somewhere I can be totally out of my depth yet still be safe, and somewhere I can experience love and awe and wonder." May this be your experience too.

Next, to encourage you, as you step out in faith, the timeless truth asserted in the Word of God in Lamentations 3:22, 23: "Because of the Lord's great love we are not consumed, for his compassions never fail. They are new every morning; great is your faithfulness." Bury these words deep in your memory, feed your soul upon them, and waking up in the morning will never be the same again!

Finally, of course, a prayer. I choose the words of Paul found in his second letter to the Thessalonians (3:5). As I select these, I am conscious that I cannot see your face and do not know your name, and so, to make the prayer a reality as I write, I call into my mind the faces of my children, whose names are written in the front of this book: "May the Lord direct your hearts into God's love and Christ's perseverance." Thus will we all one day, by his grace, see our names written in another book: the Lamb's Book of Life.

Index

Administration, gift of 105-106
Adoration (see also *Prayer*)..................................31
Adoption 16-17
Agape (see *Love*)
Anselm of Canterbury 9, 50
Answers, to prayer (see *Prayer*)
Apostles 95-96
Assurance ....Ch. 2

Baird, Catherine 73
Basics (see *Ground Rules*)
Bible (see *Scriptures*)
Body of Christ (see *Church*)
Bonhoeffer, Dietrich 69
Booth, Catherine 51, 117, 118, 130
Booth, William 51, 117, 118, 155
"Born again" 10-11
Brengle, Samuel Logan 117, 118, 161

Calvin, John 117
Career (see *Work*)
Charismatic, *charis*, etc. 81-83
Christlikeness ....57-61, Ch. 5, 118
Church 33-39, 90
Cleansing 73, 85
Cliques 39
Commitment ....Ch. 1, 35
Confession 31
Congregation, skills needed 37-39
Conversion ....Ch. 1, 109-110

Critical comment 38-39
Cross, of Jesus 6-9

Daily prayer (see *Prayer*)
Discontent, spiritual 111-112
Discouragement 41
Divine presence 3-4, 163, 166-167
Divisiveness 39, 89
Doctrine 112
Doubts 13-14

Emotions 14-15
Evangelism, gift of 141-142
Extrovert 30

Faith, gift of 102-103
Faith, living by 103
Faithfulness, a spiritual fruit 74-75
Faithfulness, of God 165-166
Family influences 36, 154
Fear 9
Feelings 14-15
First fruits 19
Forgiveness 31
Francis of Assissi 50
Friendships 46-49, 145
Fruit of the Spirit .... 60, Ch. 5, 81, 84-85, 91
Full time service (see *Vocation*)

Gauntlett, Carvosso 52
Gifts of the Spirit .... Ch. 6, Ch. 7
Glossolalia (see also *Tongues*) 100, 101
Goodness 73, 74, 77

Grace 81
Ground rules, spiritual .... Ch. 3
Growth, spiritual .... 10, Ch. 5, 168-170
Guarantee 18
Guidance, from God 155-157

Healings, gift of 103-104
Helping, gift of 105
Holiness .... 84, Ch. 8, 149, 168
Holy Spirit 15-16, 18, 19, 20, 32, 47, 49,
 .... Ch. 5, 83, 85, 89, Ch. 8

Interpretation of tongues, gift of 100-102
Intercessions (see also *Prayer*) 31
Introvert 30

Jesus (as role model) 53, 57-60
Joy 66-68

Kindness 72-73
King, Martin Luther, Jr. 52-53, 167

Leaders, Christian 37, 38, 48, 156
Love, *agape* 4, 65-66, 71, 72, 85-89, 91-93, 99, 107
Lists, of spiritual gifts in the New Testament 85-91
Luther, Martin 50, 70, 117

Martyn, Henry 162-163
Maturity, spiritual (see also *Growth*) .... Ch. 5
Meekness 75-76, 84
Mercy Seat 36, 170
Money (see also *Tithing*) .... Ch. 9

Obedience, to God ....Ch. 11, 168
Old Testament 54-55
Opportunities 40

Patience 70-71
Peace 68-60
Place of worship 33-39
Practical service (see *Service*)
Prayer 2, 27-33, 37
    –answers 32, 104, 147
    –daily 29
    –for holiness 123-124
    –petitions 31, 32
Preaching 33, 35, 28, 98, 156
Presence (see *Divine presence*)
Prophecy, gift of 90, 96-99

Reassurance ....Ch. 2
Role models ....Ch. 4, 148

Saints, New Testament meaning 113-114
Schweitzer, Albert 52
Scriptures 2, 24-27, 38, 53, 143, 155
Sealing, by the Holy Spirit 17-18
"Second blessing" 116
Self-control 77-78
Service (see also *Full time service*) 40-42
Shyness 144
Studies, as a student ....Ch. 11 (esp. 158-159)

Teaching, gift of 99
Teresa of Avila 51
Thanksgiving 31, 37

Tithing 136-138
Tongues, gift of 83, 89, 91, 100-102

Uniform, wearing 36, 149
Unity 41, 86-69

Versions, of Scripture 24-25
Vocation ....Ch. 11 (esp. 158-163)

Watson, David 97, 103
Wealth ....Ch. 9
Wesley, John 51, 117, 118
Witnessing ....Ch. 10
Work, secular ....Ch. 11
Worship (see also *Congregation; Place of worship*)........35, 37

Xenoglossia (see also *Tongues*) 100, 101